HIRE, FIRE
& THE WALKING
DEAD

A Leaders Guide to Recruiting the Best

by Greg Moran
with Patrick Longo

W **Business Books**

an imprint of New Win Publishing
a division of Academic Learning Company, LLC

ISBN: 0-8329-5001-7
Library of Congress Control Number 2006003686
Manufactured in the United States of America
10 09 08 07 06   1 2 3 4 5

Testimonials

A fast company can never truly succeed without the right people. *Hire, Fire & the Walking Dead* provides a step-by-step guide to recruiting the best. Read it, follow it and grow.

Verne Harnish
"The Growth Guru"
"One of the Top 10 small business thinkers," Fortune Small Business Magazine
Author, Mastering the Rockefeller Habits
Founder, Young Entrepreneurs Organization
CEO, Gazelles, Inc.

Greg's book is invaluable. The perspective from a real entrepreneur makes this book much more real and practical.

Jeff Behrens
Adviza Consulting

Hire, Fire & the Walking Dead pinpoints an essential element of our company's growth and success—that is, recruiting right pays!

Damon Gersh, President and CEO
Maxon's Restorations, Inc.
An Inc. 500 Company (2003)
Ernst & Young Entrepreneur of the Year (2002)

People, People, People. They will make or break your business! Greg Moran has the answers. Get it right from the start!

Brien Biondi
Executive Director, Chief Executives Organization
Former CEO, Young Entrepreneurs' Organization
2002 and 2003 National Finalist - Ernst & Young Entrepreneur of the Year Awards

Great organizations come to exist only when they find consistency in their ability to acquire top talent. Greg Moran's *Hire, Fire & the Walking Dead* presents a compelling read on why the hiring process is a management, more than HR, priority. His easy-to-follow roadmap points out many markers most hiring managers overlook as they speed down the hiring highway, guided only by their "gut"-level instincts.

Martin Babinec

Founder/President and CEO, TriNet

Inc. 500 Hall of Fame Inductee

Silicon Valley Entrepreneur of the Year

I am sincerely impressed with your ability to connect with real recruiting issues. You have skillfully outlined current and often bad practices being employed by many companies, without insulting the reader.

Robert Hayes

President and CEO

Provantage Funding Corporation

Greg Moran's recruiting advice is right on target when it comes to attracting talent into a growing organization. This book is required reading for any executive who is committed to hiring the right person the first time!

Guy Maddalone

CEO, GTM Household Employment Experts

Author, How to Hire & Retain Your Household Help

Dedication

To my three true loves:
Allison, Liv & Jack

Contents

Acknowledgments

The whole experience of writing a book is a slightly odd one. While you spend a great deal of time alone writing, it is by no means a solitary pursuit. Quite the contrary. So many people play a significant role—many without even knowing it. You know you are blessed when you have trouble listing all of the people who have been there and made this a reality. Here is my attempt at saying thank you to PT, Danny W., YEO Albany and my forum, Guy, Pat Longo, Joe Miller, Tim, Ollie, Vince, Gab, Jason, and the PA/PAA team, Martin Babinec, Verne Harnish, and Pat Lencioni, Amy and Karen from The Table Group.

Especially,

Allison
Dan & Vikki (A.K.A my parents).
Ira
Tim
Dick & Mandy

Each in a unique way, you made this possible. Thank you.

Introduction

It's been about 10 years since I entered the recruitment business. During that time, I have interviewed more than 2,000 applicants, hired hundreds and fired dozens. I have built a company of approximately 60 people. I brought a company through a significant downsizing in the wake of 9/11 and through the burst of the great tech bubble. My clients have included some of the world's largest— and some of the newest—companies. Some have been the most sophisticated in the world, and some, I must say, were appallingly naive.

Why am I telling you this? Any recruiter can share stories of utter insanity when it comes to the methods (or lack thereof) used by companies when hiring and managing their people. This book is about the lessons I learned in the trenches of the recruitment business and how you, as a business manager or entrepreneur, can apply them to build a world-class organization of top performers.

The blunt truth is that the only way to gauge the difference between poor performers and star performers may indeed be related to your own performance. You can't operate from a "same-old, same-old" perspective. What I've found is that you must be willing to look beyond the tried and (occasionally) true methodologies to find a different set of answers to well-placed questions. Rather than present example questions here, I ask that you simply read on. You will get a chance to answer many common questions throughout this book. Only by asking the right questions and seeking the right answers will you achieve consistent results from your workforce and reach your goals of having a well-compensated, productive and even happy (or at least content) team. It doesn't take an expert to know this means higher revenue.

It's unfortunate that, at some point, we all fear the regulatory issues of hiring or that interacting with our employees can jeopardize our business in some way. But you must remember that hiring, developing, coaching and retaining employees are what separate success from failure in any business or human resource department. What many people fail to realize is that a large percentage of businesses don't have a human resource department; thus, people who have no real training perform all inherent functions of this department.

It is my hope that I can provide you with some ideas to develop a sound, proven recruiting strategy. This means there will be fewer problems for you, and you will have the foresight to keep it that way. You will be more proactive than reactive and confident that any small glitch can be fixed with a little common sense, creativity and good, old-fashioned elbow grease. This is because you will have the knowledge it takes to be confident. But before we begin, there are a few ground rules—or small, distinct realities—that you need to realize and accept if you are to learn anything from this book.

First, I am *not* a human resource professional. I do not have any formal training in the administrative or regulatory components of the human resource business. I am an entrepreneur who has fought many battles and learned a lot of hard-won lessons in HR. If you work in a large organization, be sure to consult your HR team for guidance before implementing some of the ideas contained in this book. Like it or not, we function in a highly litigious business environment these days, and personnel matters are among the first targets, which is only compounding the problems faced by employers. We always seem to be on the defensive, when we really should just have a solid, well-thought-out offense.

Second, I do not have all the answers, not that you necessarily thought I did. This book is about getting you to ask some important questions regarding your ability to build your single most expensive business asset: your workforce. These questions will lead you down a path of creative and innovative methodology to attract the best people, hire them and make them winners. If you do not find the "answers" in this book, then I will be happy to know that you were prompted by the material presented here to find them.

Lastly, I am not a writer by trade. Entrepreneurship *is* my business. Currently, I am involved in another startup company that markets the world's leading technology for pre-employment assessment and employee development. Like you, my days are filled with trying to attract, screen and develop people who have the ability and burning desire to be the best. Like you, I have failed and will likely fail again in this effort. But I continue to learn from my successes, as well as my failures. The "people business" is not an exact science. It is difficult, inconsistent and disappointing at times. But just like everything else in this world, it is *never* hopeless.

That's my bit about me. So much of this "people business" is about common sense and the ability to recognize that whether you're a CEO or the front-desk receptionist, humans are humans and will usually demand to be treated that way. Companies that do so will be rewarded; companies that do not will likely fail. It really is that simple. What goes around comes around, and I personally want the good to come around.

Before we begin, let me leave you with a closing comment. Think. There it is. Think of how and when you perform at your best. Think of the differences among you and your friends and how nonsensical it is to treat everyone the same and expect the same results. Think of the best job or boss you've had. What made the difference? Who would you like to thank in your great award speech or at your retirement party?

This book is about the individual pursuit of excellence and how we, as managers of an enlightened workforce, must foster this reality. There is an old saying in business: "You manage machines and lead people." Let's begin to lead, from the right place, and free our people to perform as they—and we—expect.

Chapter 1
It's Not HR's Fault

Chapter 1
It's Not HR's Fault

Just as with any self-help topic, volumes of useless, wildly overengineered books have been written on recruiting. Maybe "useless" is a bit too harsh, but "theoretical" and "impractical" may be a better description. Recruiting top talent is not that hard to figure out. You and your company are probably executing the behaviors necessary—today —to successfully recruit without even thinking about it. These behaviors are called "selling," and they are virtually identical to recruiting. The product is different, and success is manifested in a much different way, but the path to success is the same.

Analogy to the Sales Process

Think about your sales process. As sales executives, we love to include anything that sounds or seems scientific. After removing many of the sales complexities, it basically works like this:

Define the Market

You have to know what you're selling, and you have to know your target market.

When recruiting talent, you must precisely identify the ideal characteristics suited to, or required for, the position for which you are hiring.

This means you need to completely understand the type of person you need inside and out. If you don't understand it, that's fine. Just find someone who does and pick their brain for all it's worth. Once you truly understand the position, you have to know your competition for the most talented applicants. Who else is hunting for the same type of candidate? Move beyond the obvious. Get to know what your market typically offers a candidate of the caliber you're seeking. Use all of the resources you can get your hands on. Use the Internet, staffing agencies, your HR department, peers in other companies— you get the point. Find the information and use it. This part will define your ability to succeed in moving forward.

Position the Product

The market will never know your product exists without clear differentiation, a message, a brand promise and a great elevator pitch. The same is true with candidates for a particular job. As a hiring manager, your primary product is career opportunity. You must break through the clutter of the job market so that top candidates notice you and will want to work for you. Stop thinking, for one moment, about what they can offer you and think about what you can offer them. Believe me when I say that money is not always the key. Be creative, and look at the value you can offer as an employer. Interview people in your company. Ask them what attracted them to you. What is not being offered that can be?

Identify your value proposition and message, and prepare to deliver it flawlessly—and often. You must break through the clutter.

Prospect, Prospect, Prospect

Would you ever let a salesperson wait until the pipeline is dry to start identifying future prospects? Of course not. But we do it all the time in recruitment. You can't bank on the fact that candidates are going to come to you because you are a wonderful company to work for. Even the greatest, most desirable, most successful companies can't do that. In sales, there are hunters, farmers and fishermen. Don't be a fisherman, waiting in the same spot and hoping to catch a fish. Simply banking on your charm and good looks is not enough. We must keep the pipeline robust and constantly recruit. Otherwise, you are banking on luck and bad luck equals desperation hiring. Recruiting takes work, and you must prospect where your competition is not looking.

It's much like determining a football lineup. If you have an aging, ailing linebacker, you probably should have been actively recruiting two to three years before his imminent demise. Don't wait until someone runs lame in your company. Look for the signs, and be ready to put in a replacement. Always be prospecting so you are ready to close when necessary—not when you are desperate.

Qualify

Not every deal is a good deal. True sales professionals know that success comes from creating an emotional desire for the product. Think of the big, archetypal, fancy clubs in Manhattan that drape a velvet rope across their door. You are looking to create exclusivity by accepting nothing but the best, and soon enough people will know it. We want what we can't have, and we are curious as to what really happens behind the doors of the chocolate factory. The best possible scenario is to have a "members only" environment that is special and unique. Success in recruiting comes from raising the bar. Exclusivity breeds desire, especially from those who want to be the best, those who measure themselves against the best and those who will drive harder to be part of something greater than themselves.

 Desire breeds better people by attracting better people.

Close

According to Alec Baldwin's character in the movie Glengarry Glen Ross, "Coffee is for closers." In other words, to the victor go the spoils. If you can't close, you lose. In recruitment, if you attract the best candidates, but lack the ability to land them consistently, you're wasting your time. Why get them to the table when you can't get them to buy? This means you can't put up a bunch of smoke and mirrors, letting them slip past the rope only to see that you're serving a keg of Meister Brau and fake cheese in a can. You have taken the deal this far, so don't lose it now.

Just as with selling, the model is easy to understand. But without consistent, systematic execution, success will never be within your reach. You have to follow the system and execute. You probably say this to your salespeople on a daily basis—and now I'm telling you to do the same thing.

The Recruitment Process

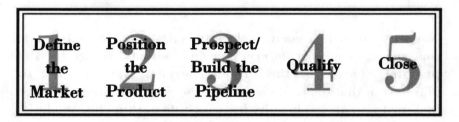

Define the Market | Position the Product | Prospect/Build the Pipeline | Qualify | Close

Line Manager Accountability

As fun as it is to blame HR for all of our problems, it is not necessarily their fault. All managers must accept responsibility and accountability for the hiring process and consequent hiring decisions. This means managing your current workforce effectively, rather than waiting for HR to set up your next round of interviews.

Just think for a moment about how HR operates. Your average recruiter may be working on five to ten different positions at any one time, all requiring different qualifications. Equate this to sales. What if your salespeople were trying to sell into five to ten markets at once? Would they have any chance to deliver results? Certainly not. They'd be spread way too thin and could not concentrate on any one particular market. Even good salespeople who stay true to one market will have a problem if they don't concentrate on a select group of similar prospects. Even most professional recruiters will focus on one market. And writers will focus on one genre. It's not an accident, a coincidence of the universe or a government conspiracy. It's common sense—tried, true, tested and proven.

The only hope an overworked, thinly spread recruiter has in this situation is to stumble across the perfect candidate. (Or better yet, the off-chance that a candidate will find him at exactly the right moment.) Is this possible? Absolutely. But do you want to bet your career on it? I would hope not. If your energy and resources are divided equally, none of your positions is an absolute, concrete priority, and you are going to fail miserably. The practical reality is that you, the manager, are best suited to recruit for your needs. It makes logical sense to stop delegating responsibility to people who are not qualified or not focused on your exact needs. This means that each manager should be taking full responsibility for the recruiting and hiring process.

The Only Thing You Can Control

One of the most frustrating aspects of managing people is that you can't always control your staff's behavior. There are light to heavy threats, micromanagement and many other completely unproductive tactics that may temporarily alter people's actions and attitudes, but in the end, the behavior usually resumes—either fully or to a degree that is still completely unacceptable.

Let me share a brief anecdote. A sixty pound English bulldog named Cigar lives with me in my home. Please notice that I did not call him "my dog." This is because he is clearly my wife's dog—and hers alone. Every time I try to walk him, he decides he has exercised enough and parks himself in the middle of a busy street. I yell. I speak nicely. I gently tug. Then I drag his butt across the road. Finally, I realized that he controls his behavior, and I don't. I am not his master. Want to know my solution? Tell my wife to walk him and get myself another dog. For sanity's sake, it is the only real option.

This is also your only answer. You have very limited influence on your current staff when it comes to deep-rooted institutional behaviors that have been developed and accepted. Your ability to recruit high potentials, though, is totally under your control. Exercise this authority and build the team that can perform. Soon enough, the others will have to match the new behaviors or fall hopelessly behind. Taking control makes all the difference.

> If you have to, create a velvet-rope scenario in your department. Strive for the exclusivity that others will want to match.

The Biggest Sale

When I first started in sales, I encountered a vice president who had a mantra that sticks with me to this day: "Focus on the activities closest to the dollar." As a sales manager, there is no activity closer to the dollar than recruiting. Talent brings money (revenue), and great talent brings great amounts of money—especially if you've done your homework and selected the person who was absolutely perfect for the job. Do this and you will bring money to your business—and money can fix most problems.

Here's a quick test for you:

1. What is your average ticket sale?
2. What does a top-performing salesperson produce for you in revenue annually?
3. Which is larger?
4. What would one more top performer do to your quota?

Get the picture? Let your salespeople deal with item number one. You should follow the big dollars and focus on the large sale, which is your talent. This is something you can control.

Figure 2-2
Sales Value Calculator

What is the most important sale that a company can make? Enter the numbers below to assess the dollar value of a top performer's sale.

On average, what amount does a top performer deliver in revenue?

$ _____

What is your average ticket sale?

$ _____

The difference between these two numbers listed above is:

$ _____

Chapter 2
Define the Market

Chapter 2
Define the Market

I have often invested in start-up companies and have rejected bad deals with equal frequency. Based on experience, what makes or breaks a deal for me is whether an entrepreneur has identified with whom they are selling. Anytime a hopeful entrepreneur utters the words "everybody needs this product," the deal is off. This simply is not true. I like to look at the little picture, see who truly needs a product, decide how to make it appealing and determine how to reach them. It's like having someone say, "Trust me." There is just no need for trust when the fit is right from the start.

Define the Market

Unfortunately, too many salespeople believe that anyone can buy their product. The end result is a constantly shifting approach and message with no clear focus. Ultimately, frustration, blame and turnover ensue. You'll find that recruiting works in the same manner. You can have a very clear target, but it is not always easy to stay focused. Finding, hiring and retaining talent are never easy. Finding the right people is challenging enough.

The hard reality is that only a very select number of individuals will become top performers in your organization. They are select because they share intangible characteristics that make them successful. Your ability to clearly identify and understand these key characteristics will determine your ability to attract top performers to your company. This task can be extremely subjective and, therefore, extremely difficult. Remember:

I am focusing on the "intangible." You cannot touch it, smell it, hear it or taste it, but you need to know it well enough to sense it.

At this point, what you're sensing is only a vague shadow, and through real diligence you will flesh out a black and white figure that clearly appears to be your next top performer.

With virtually all of the clients with whom I deal, the search begins and ends with hard skills, such as the ability to cold-call, set up meetings, close, etc. Many recruiters think previous sales expertise in selling techno-widgets and other innumerable products is the Holy Grail of top-performer identification. Forget it. This is usually not the case. While it may provide insight into one facet of the candidate's profile, it is not always indicative of top-performing sellers. True success factors result from other, softer and much harder-to-identify areas of the individual's total profile. I am referring to an individual's "IPC" makeup.

The IPC

IPC stands for Intellect, Personality and Cultural fit—the success factors that truly matter.

Explore these characteristics in a person, and you will expose something far more critical. You will identify what this person was practically born to do. You may chuckle to yourself when you hear this, and I somewhat want to laugh right along with you, but I need to ask you this: Have you ever done something that just felt right? Were you asked to do an assignment or project, and it just "clicked"? You're half-thinking, "Man, that was fun. I could do this all day and not even feel as though I was working!" Who knows why? It just felt right. This is how your IPC profile should manifest before your eyes. It is the perfect alignment of your mental horsepower, your personality and your environmental needs, along with the task at hand.

Top performers in any given job within your company share the right profile with their position in the company. You rarely, if ever, have a problem, and the person is happy as a clam and performing consistently well. This is because the perfect alignment doesn't depend on skills or experience alone. Chances are, if you ask a top performer to do the same job at a different company, he/she may flounder or even fail completely. The true explanation: You changed one of the factors. We call this the cultural fit.

In poker terms, skills are the table stakes. Skills are simply the cost to enter the game and sit at the table. They mean little when determining how much you win in the long run.

Let's take a closer look at "I," "P" and "C."

Intellect

What intellectual capacity do top performers share? I am not referring to IQ necessarily, but rather the employee's ability to process, analyze and communicate information. I can appreciate that we all have different intelligence factors. Some people process information slowly and deliberately before drawing any conclusions. This doesn't make them less intelligent than one who thinks fast and/or one who speaks even faster. I can speak gibberish, but fast-talking or fast-communicating does not necessarily equal gibberish.

Remember the old Fed-Ex ad with the guy who could speak so ridiculously fast, yet you could actually understand him? The guy who soon parlayed this ability into his fifteen minutes and played himself out in the market? That's a great skill, but it's not going to get you a customer service job anytime soon—and other than ad sales on TV, it's not going to get you a sales job anytime soon, either. Consider Albert Einstein. Smart enough guy, right? Would you want him working customer service for your company? Why not? He would over-engineer the position, treat your customers like idiots and become hopelessly bored. Remember: We are not talking about hiring the smartest person; rather, we need the "right" level of intelligence compared to the job's requirements. There are many factors that need to align for you to assign an intelligence measure to certain skills or behaviors, such as verbal skills, numerical skills and overall mental aptitude.

When considering the cognitive skills of a top performer, think about verbal and numerical issues separately.

Some people work well with numbers, but have great trouble communicating them—and vice versa. Do you have an open position that requires both skills at the same time? For a top performer in any position, you may need a person who can demonstrate both—but not necessarily. Each position can be geared toward certain intelligences or a mix of several. You need to be a keen observer and clearly identify the attributes of top performers in your company. Do this for every position, and you are on your way to filling your pool with top talent across the board.

I want to offer a firm word of caution here. All too often, I see companies claim that they "only want the smartest." Believe me when I say that this is an ego-driven statement that will, in the long run, cause many problems. Intellectual people often fail in inappropriate jobs because they are simply too theoretical and do not think according to the position for which they are hired—and they fail miserably. It sounds great to say that we hire only the smartest people. Look how smart you sound just saying it! But your ego will beat you every time on this one. You must hire people whose intellect matches your top people doing this job today—nothing more or less. It's all relative. If you want to look smart, wash your clothing in 50% more detergent and only drive your car on a closed track with a professional driver. Don't try to make your workforce something it is not and shouldn't be.

Let me give an example to clarify my point. I once had a client who hired programmers by the dozen. One manager within the organization decided that he would only hire candidates with off-the-charts IQs and GPAs. He would publicly and proudly proclaim that he would only accept the smartest. On the surface, it's pretty hard to argue with this logic. But here's the problem: This manager could

r a project on time to save his life. Can you speculate on em with this IQ dream team? His programmers became h following the process, and independently decided to code er their part of the project in a different and "better" way.

ιsiness Books

For this manager, this meant that all standards and processes were gone. His people were extremely bright, but they couldn't work as a team and execute according to the process. Budgets were constantly exceeded, deadlines were missed and customers were furious.

Good examples of the opposite scenario are seemingly limitless. All too often, people who communicate and interview extremely well find themselves in a position that doesn't suit their intellect. This is often the case when recruiting high-end salespeople. The assumption that a great salesperson can sell anything is nonsense. Look at salespeople who sell high-ticket items that are more transactional in nature (i.e., cars, homes, etc.). When placed in a very complex, long-cycle selling situation, they can quickly lose their way because this type of sale requires totally different skills and behaviors. Are they less intelligent than their peers? Maybe, maybe not. It doesn't matter. What matters is the manner in which their minds work. This is the wrong selling environment for them, and you just helped turn an A-player into a D-player for your company.

To complete this section, rate your top performers' ability to process and communicate (express) verbal and numerical information on a scale of one to ten. Consider both speed and accuracy when you are making this judgment, as they are both of critical importance. Once you've ranked your top performers, consider your bottom performers and rank them in the same manner. Do you see any differences? If not, it's OK. They will emerge later, under even greater scrutiny.

Personality

Which personality traits do top performers share? Our personality in the workplace is defined by our everyday behavioral characteristics, such as ambition, emotional stability, extroversion and numerous other inherent behaviors.

We are not going to overdo it here. For the next page, just think about these top performers and list the characteristics you believe they currently have, or have had, in common. Were they outgoing or introverted? Were they very energetic and dynamic or more contemplative? Again, be careful to answer truthfully—not how you feel it should be or want it to be. For this section, you need to be very objective—and humans are anything but objective. We are just not built for it.

 Don't let your emotions and biases negate your objectivity.

Also examine the bottom performers. Make sure you let go of any water-cooler feuds that will color your opinions. Describe the elements of their personality objectively. Are the differences between the two groups clearly starting to emerge now? Chances are, the clouds are clearing, and the picture is more evident—more black and white. If not, the position itself may be a little gray and require further review. For now, let's get to what many people consider to be the most important criterion: the cultural fit.

Cultural

Every business has a unique set of mores and attitudes that exist, regardless of whether we have defined them. (Just because we haven't named it doesn't mean it fails to exist.) Without a doubt, more than with any other criterion, bad matches are made because there is a poor cultural fit. A great individual performer may go to work for a good company, but it just doesn't "click," and it's sometimes difficult to figure out why. In reality, it's usually caused by a cultural mismatch—an IBM "suit" going to work for a Berkeley-based dot.com. Your ability to accurately assess your culture, and to appropriately and effectively screen for this criterion, will immediately impact your hiring performance.

Now, let's go back to your list of top performers and answer the eight questions on the following page. Rate them according to the provided matrix. Then complete the same task for your bottom performers. Do you see the difference? These three areas (intellect, behavior and cultural fit), when combined with the more obvious inventory of hard skills, will provide the best roadmap to your hiring success. The exercise you just completed, while fairly rudimentary, is a great starting point. By using the benchmark of your top performers as a target, you have a measuring stick for any new hires. Use this stick to evaluate top candidates, as well as B- and C-players, and you will start to "know" and "see" an A-player. You'll be able to spot a C-player immediately because he looks nothing like the A-player you have in your head.

Figure 4-3

Cultural Fit Profiler

Use this worksheet to determine the culture in which your top performers are excelling. Read each of the following eight questions
and rate your organization on the provided scale.

Do not rate where you want to be; rather, be brutally honest about where you are today.

Make copies of the worksheet and provide them to a sampling of
your top performers. Compare the results. Do you see any differences? If so, discuss them with the respondents and try to reconcile
the gaps.

1.) Business Attitude: A conventional business culture relies
on traditional philosophies and strategies, resists progressive
notions, and approaches situations conservatively. A progressive business culture is open to new ideas, welcomes change
and embraces innovative approaches.

1	2	3	4	5
+ Relies on traditional policies	+ Promotes conventional thought	+ Typically operates convention-ally	+Seeks new ideas and strategies	+ Rewards risk and innovation
- Opposed to change	- Many times, overly conventional	- May miss a progressive opportunity	- Often overlooks conventional wisdom	- Resists conventional thought

Conventional   Progressive

2.) Change: A stable culture reflects consistency day in and day out, dislikes change and enjoys a daily routine. A changing culture embraces change as positive, asks workers to adapt easily and promotes diversity.

1	2	3	4	5
+ Predictable environment	+ Keeps workable solutions	+ Makes needed adjustments	+ Encourages quality changes	+ Is perpetually adjusting
- Nonproductive when change occurs	- Responds to change slowly	- May not appropriately adjust to changing demands	- Overly focused on changes	- Nonproductive adjustments are made

Stable   Changing

3.) Competitiveness: A supportive culture puts others first, asks employees to make adjustments to others and avoids conflict. A competitive culture has competition for incentives, strong promotion of the need to win and frequent conflict present in the culture.

1	2	3	4	5
+ Assists without competition	+Promotes accomodating others	+ Mix of support and competition	+ Values competition	+ Wins at all costs
- Resists competition; prefers supporting	- Downplays personal needs	-Does not fully capture the essence of competition or support	- May overlook others' needs	- Competes at the expense of others

Supportive   Competitive

4.) Job Atmosphere: A relaxed culture promotes fun in the workplace, attracts playful employees, and reflects a casual environment. A serious environment focuses solely on business, spends no time on fun activities and has a low tolerance for play.

1	2	3	4	5
+ Spontaneous atmosphere	+Playful, casual and relaxed	+ Takes work seriously, but relaxed	+ Reflects seriousness and formality	+ Very serious and formal
- Overly playful; at times non-productive	- Often, too casual; lacks seriousness	- Play could show at wrong times	- Uptight; often too formal	- Overly serious; not spontaneous enough

Relaxed   Serious

5.) Organizational Structure: An unstructured environment has a loose reporting structure, has few if any guidelines and values flexibility in the workplace. A structured culture has a clear line of authority, requires strict adherence to company regulations and appears more formal in its practices and procedures.

1	2	3	4	5
+ Ability to move in many directions	+ Flexible guidelines	+ Average amount of structure	+ Provides structure to employees	+ Clear, precise expectations
- No guildelines or parameters	- Does not provide enough direction	- At times, overly structured	- Over reliance on company policies	- Missed opportunities due to no zero flexibility

Unstructured   Structured

6.) Pace: A slow-paced environment produces work slowly and steadily, reflects a lower energy level and focuses on one task at a time. A fast-paced environment has a sense of urgency, is action-oriented and involves multiple tasks on a daily basis.

1	2	3	4	5
+ Steady pace; focused activities	+ Not deadline-oriented	+ Average pace, according to the situation	+ Sense of urgency	+ High rate of speed
- Operates too slowly	- Non responsive to crisis	- May adopt the wrong pace	- May speed by past important data points	- Often impatient and scattered

Slow-Paced   **Fast-Paced**

7.) Social Contact: An infrequent social culture does not require attendance to social events, does not provide structured social activities, but emphasizes and focuses on the task aspects of work. An environment that provides frequent social contact plans parties and social gatherings regularly, incorporates social gatherings with the tasks at work and enjoys social interaction.

1	2	3	4	5
+ Work focused	+ Will not be distracted by socializing	+ Socializing in modera-tion	+ Provides social opportunities	+ Daily social interaction opportunity
- Disre-gards social events	- Devalues social interactions	- Tired of excessive social interaction	- Socializing may overshadow task completion	- Inhibits performance

Infrequent Social Contacts   **Frequent**

8.) Stress: A low-stress culture encompasses few stressful activities, lacks direct or perceived pressure and possesses a low degree of responsibility. A high-stress culture involves timelines in pressure situations, requires a high tolerance for anxiety and involves external and internal job pressures.

1	2	3	4	5
+No pressure	+Lower degree of responsibility	+ Invloves occasional stress	+External and internal job pressures	+Pressure and stress on a daily basis
- No motivation	- Low initiative	-Difficult in extreme stress	- Disregards emotional stress	- May burn out employees

Low Stress   High Stress

Skills Assessment

All positions demand a certain amount of required knowledge. If you are hiring a nurse, you'll want some knowledge of medicine. However, most companies set the skills standards excruciatingly high, as with a nurse who can take over and operate on a trauma patient's ruptured spleen. As a result, the talent pool becomes entirely too small, and we are forced to choose between candidates who may not fit the IPC profile. This is like going to the prom with your last choice because you were waiting for the Homecoming King/Queen to ask you out. Most companies either set the bar too high or too low. We need to focus on getting it right.

When determining required skills, stick to the basic; remember that training is always an option if you are hiring for talent.

Resist the temptation to load up on "nice-to-haves" and rigidly stick to the "must-haves." Since we are talking about "must-haves" here, it would be a good idea to eliminate some of them, as well, if you are looking to tone down your skills focus and find the right overall

(IPC) match for your company. We are looking for individuals who are "meant" to do this job.

Ideal Candidate Profile: Summary

Combine your IPC characteristics and hard skills, and you will have your Ideal Profile. Congratulations! You now have your target. Continue to follow the worksheet to help you further compile this information.

The Ideal Profile Summary

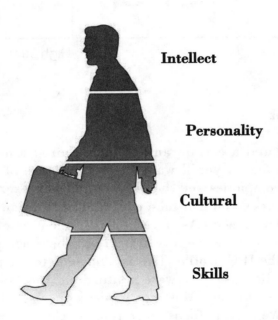

Intellect

Personality

Cultural

Skills

**Figure 5-3
"Defining the Target" Exercise**

Think of the individual you have hired who best embodies a top performer. This may be a current or past hire.

Fold this paper into thirds. Then answer the questions in each of the three boxes. Copy this page and distribute it to others. Compare answers. Look for similarities in the profile created by each participant.

Intellect

Intellectually, what made this person successful? Good with numbers, verbal skills, analytical, quick thinking, etc.?

Personality

Which adjectives best describe this individual's personality? Motivated, high-energy, outgoing, calm, etc.?

Cultural Fit

What about this person made him/her fit into the culture? Dealt well with stress, focused on task at hand, worked at a fast pace?

Competitive Landscape: Identifying the Talent Pool

Now that you have your Ideal Profile under control, you are on your way. We now need to understand our competition. This is absolutely critical in any selling situation, including recruitment. But you must change your thinking about your competition. Your competition for talent includes your business competitors, as well as other organizations with whom you do not compete for business. You must identify organizations seeking the same type of talent as yours—not merely those that sell the same product/service or those whose potential eats into your revenues. Keep in mind that certain hard skills may have nothing to do with your top performer for each position.

 Understanding your competition for talent may take a good amount of research, but you need to become familiar with some unknown territory if you are to excel at this.

One of my clients is in the advertising business, and his company has a very unique product targeted to new homeowners. He has several competitors—businesses like his—that also target this demographic. When it's time to recruit, competition for candidates increases because his business only employs salespeople on 100% commission. This means he is clearly trying to pull talent from his traditional competitors (those in the ad business), as well as realtors, insurance and financial sales organizations, auto dealers and countless other companies in his region that target salespeople willing to work for 100% commission. These companies are seeking the same people my client wishes to employ; therefore differentiation becomes critical. I will talk about this later in more detail, but please know that understanding your competition is vital to your ability to successfully position your "product." The following competitor analysis worksheet will help you sort this out before moving on to "Positioning Your Product."

Figure 6-3

Talent Competitor Worksheet
Answer the questions below to determine your main competitors for the talent you need. Do not limit yourself solely to business competitors.

1.) Hard Skills
Are there any hard-skills requirements that must be sought for a potential hire? (Note: For a discussion of hard skills, refer to Chapter 3 on the IPC profile.)

2.) Tasks
What are the required routine tasks or characteristics of the position? (Examples: transactional selling, closing, cold-calling, fielding support calls, managing support team, etc.)

3.) Compensation
How is this position compensated? (Examples: 100% commission, high base plus performance incentives, all salary/no performance, 1099 contractor status?)

4.) Geographic Range
Where are these candidates located? Are there many in my local area, or will they need to be recruited elsewhere?

5.) Possible Competitors Based on Above?

Talent Competitor Worksheet Sample

Position: Automobile Sales

1.) Hard Skills
Aptitude for selling and service. Fast with numbers and financial terminology.

2.) Tasks
Transactional selling, closing, good follow-up. Ability to deal with rejection.

3.) Compensation
100% commission with other performance incentives.

4.) Geographic Range
Local geography.

5.) Possible Competitors Based on Above
Financial service sales (insurance, stock brokerage), real estate sales, media/advertising sales, other car dealerships, boat/RV dealerships.

Define the Market: Summary

What's the biggest sale your organization can make? Hiring a future top performer. Your hiring managers must accept this reality and prepare themselves in the same manner that your organization prepares its sales force. You can begin this process by defining the target candidate using the Ideal Profile. Made up of Intellect, Personality and Cultural Fit—as well as skills, to a lesser degree—the Ideal Profile will become your yardstick for measuring candidates against your current top performers. Indeed, this too can actually help you pinpoint weaknesses in your current staff and take steps to correct them.

The intellect measure will answer the question: "Can they do the job?" The behavioral measure answers: "Will they do the job?" The cultural measure tells you if they will "raise the bar" for those around them. The Ideal Profile will become your primary source for candidate identification and evaluation. Be certain, at this point, that the skills identified for the position are "must-haves" and not "nice-to-haves" (or even "rather-haves").

Lastly, understand the competitive landscape. In other words, get to know all of the other options available to potential candidates. This may include your standard business competitors or other organizations, as mentioned previously. When you feel you understand your "product" and your product competitors, you are ready to move on to the next step: "Positioning the Product."

Chapter 3
Positioning the Product

Chapter 3
Positioning the Product

If your customers cannot figure out where you and your product fit in the marketplace, you're in deep trouble. This is because they are relying on you to tell them. You may think this sounds like a shady, propagandist viewpoint, but it's the simple truth. Anyone who has ever sold anything can confirm it. The customer's visceral understanding of how you align with his needs—versus the other options available to him—is critical. Remember: Simplicity is genius. You need to figure this out, get customers' attention in a blazing mass of competitive white noise, and tell them your story quickly, succinctly, accurately and passionately (or just run a cool, really funny Super Bowl ad and hope they line up at your door).

The same premise holds true when attracting and acquiring talent. If your message doesn't clearly define who you are and why you should be given strong consideration as an employer, you will be lumped in with everyone else. In the cluster of noisy recruitment marketplaces, prospective candidates will get lost and never find you. It's like the food vendors in the mall: they all want you to sample a piece of flavored chicken on a stick so you'll opt to buy your lunch from their booths. What could possibly be so different about any one of those chicken clumps on a stick? Not much. They all look pretty much the same to the average guy passing by.

You need to create a unique message that is communicated flawlessly on a consistent basis. Once your unique message has been created, your "salespeople" must then be prepared and fully trained to deliver it, and to add value to the message when necessary. This takes some flexibility, of course, but you don't want it to get too messy.

Without a clearly defined strategy to deliver your message to potential candidates, you are losing out on critical leads that will keep your pipeline full.

The primary product of any sales manager today (or any line manager who heavily relies on recruiting talent) is career opportunity. Many companies treat the candidate recruitment process in a reactive manner. While focusing all of their time on selling the next widget, they forget that part of their role in the company is to always be recruiting the next A-player/widget-seller. If you missed this point before, return to Chapter 1. Use the supplied calculator, give it to your managers, and see if it gets their attention.

Differentiation

What if you had a sales rep who consistently bungled his opening sales pitch everywhere he went? And what if I told you that he not only stumbled through an incoherent message, but the words he actually managed to spit out were inconsistent and contradictory? Wouldn't you sit down next to him and mutually decide that it may be time for some training? I would think so.

I may be guessing here, but I'll bet that if I asked your sales managers why a career opportunity at your company is the right move, their answers would vary...wildly. Most organizations are simply not prepared to "sell" opportunities at their companies and wind up fumbling like our hapless sales rep. Again, we tend to focus on the widget-selling and not on the "closest-to-the-dollar activity": finding the next star widget-seller.

Differentiation is all about getting to the heart of the matter and answering the question "why?" *Why* should I work for you? *Why* are you different, special or exciting? In short, *why* should I fully commit myself to you and your mission for the next five years of my life, rather than signing on with the other ten companies calling on me, telling me how special they are and explaining why they warrant my loyalty for those same five years? These are tough questions to answer if you're not prepared, and they catch most companies off guard time and time again.

The worksheet on differentiation will help you fully develop the answers to these questions: Why are you special? What do you have to offer that is unique and difficult for other companies to match? Chances are, if people continue to work for you, there are some clear differentiators, many of which you may not be aware of, even from seasoned employees. Have you ever thought to ask? You may have. On the other hand, many other issues you take for granted on a daily basis are difficult to see.

Think about your organization. What attracted you to it in the first place? Let's look again at my commission-only advertising client. Flexibility defined him. If a candidate is a stay-at-home parent who wants to deliver the kids to the bus each morning and be there when the children come home, this company may offer an ideal employment opportunity. The company has built a culture around this type of employee and is able to leverage this benefit in its messaging. When the company breaks through the clutter and captures a candidate's attention, it has that message clearly stamped on its collective corporate forehead. So, what are the things that define *you*? Here's a tip:

Ask your current top performers why they chose you. Also ask them what motivates them to stay, and look for the similarities and patterns in their answers. These are your differentiators.

Like a salesperson, make sure you ask the right questions in the right manner so you get the most honest answers. People don't like to be probed.

Some of your messaging may be job-specific (high commission, etc.) and some may be company-specific (flexibility, etc.). You need a balance of the two, with a greater emphasis on the *company* side. After all, the job is what *grabs* someone initially, but the company is what *keeps* them. A company-culture fit is the greatest differentiator and attractor of talent. A poor match sets you up for failure.

Start working on this now by using the differentiation worksheet. Make sure your top performers contribute to this part of the process, as it's a lot easier to define potential A-players if you match them with a profile developed by your existing A-players. Their contribution is the key to moving to the next step: creating the "elevator pitch."

Figure 7-4

Differentiation Worksheet

Copy and distribute this form to all of your top performers by job category (i.e., sales, customer service, management, etc.). Ask each top performer to complete it and return it to you. What are the common answers among the responses? Bring a sampling of respondents together, and discuss the findings. Fully dive into the issues.

1.) Originally, why did you choose to work for this company?

2.) What are the top three factors that have facilitated your success in your current position?

3.) What do you feel differentiates this organization from others for whom you could work?

4.) What would you tell a prospective hire about this company?

Elevator Pitch

The elevator pitch is as old as sales itself. If you are unfamiliar with the term, it refers to the practice of pitching your story in the limited amount of time it takes an elevator to reach its destination—not a very long time for those who have somehow evaded this scenario in the past. It is high-pressure selling at its best. If you cannot get someone's attention in the elevator, he'll be gone, and the elevator will move on. This requires a precise, well-delivered message, as well as actual practice, because you rarely get to pitch in an actual elevator! There are many instances where you can deliver this pitch, and each may require a slight variation to accommodate particular scenarios.

This concept is especially potent in a networking situation. For example, if you attend a chamber of commerce function, charity event, trade show or other fast-moving "sales situation," you may have only about 20 seconds to develop interest in opportunities within your company. A high-impact elevator pitch is mandatory in recruitment, as well as sales. Before you can deliver this "pitch," you need to develop the message so it can be delivered consistently. Keep it simple. Use the differentiators you established in the previous section. After all, what matters more than what your top performers think?

Once you have settled on the differentiators, choose the best of them and create a statement that concisely answers why someone should work for you. Here's an example:

Differentiators:

Flexibility to support stay-at-home parents
Uncapped earning potential
Full benefits in a commission-only role

Elevator Pitch:

"XYZ Company provides the chance for a completely flexible workday, based on your personal needs, with the uncapped earning potential our top people demand. We further support our people with one of the industry's only full-benefits pack-ages for commission-only reps."

This may be a little tight and bland for certain situations (such as a request for a referral), but you should get the idea. If not, study it once again, and create it with the help of your top performers to ensure you hit all of the emotional impact available in such a short period.

If you were in the target group for this company, would your radar be up after hearing this pitch? Most likely, yes. Notice the qualifier: "If you were in the target group." We are not writing this to tell the world how great we are. (We'll discuss that later, when we talk about PR.) We are pitching the individual standing before us: a possible candidate. This is hand-to-hand (or, as a friend says, belly-to-belly) selling at its best. Be prepared with a clear and, most importantly, meaningful message, and you will gain the edge over your competi-tion. Fumble now and candidates walk away—always remembering the fumble, not the sweet pass you catch in the playoffs the follow-ing year. Do you want the highlight film goofs or the Super Bowl ring? It's your choice.

 Use the elevator pitch worksheet to practice creating a mes-sage for your target group.

The words you use are important, but your delivery is equally crit-ical. Get the message down, spread it around the office, get comfort-able with it and practice it. Practice it in front of a mirror. Record yourself. Videotape it. Role-play it in your weekly meeting. Whatever you do, make sure you know it inside and out—and that you believe it. It's hard to stand by even the most earnest lie. Know it inside and out because you'll be using it a lot.

Elevator Pitch Exercise

Before beginning, make sure you have completed the exercise on differentiation. Refresh your memory on the answers provided by your top performers, as they will be the basis for this exercise.

1.) When reviewing the answers provided on the differentiation exercise, what are the five most common themes identified from all of the questions?

2.) Frame these themes into a ten second "pitch" that captures the differentiators. Be sure to be as conversational as possible.

Figure 8-4 Continued

Elevator Pitch Sample

1.) Common Themes:

- Company's long history
- Company's successful track record
- Flexible hours based on your lifestyle
- No cap on earnings
- Protected territories

2.) Elevator Pitch:

XYZ Company is always looking for high-potential talent. We have a long and successful performance history, as well as a culture that supports flexibility based on your lifestyle needs. We place no cap on earnings in a protected sales territory. If you or someone you know is interested, please call me.

Brand Promise

What does Southwest Airlines promise to give its customers at all times, no matter what? How about the NY Yankees? If you said low fares and fun service for the first question and a winning baseball team for the second, you're right. A brand promise is the expressed or implied statement of what a business will do for its customers over and over again. It represents consistency in the eyes of consumers and keeps them coming back for more.

Gregory's is a barbershop I frequent in Albany, NY (the name is just a coincidence). Every time I get my hair cut, a friendly face greets me at the front desk in the same, pleasant manner. The reception area is always clean, and the stylists are extremely professional and communicate with ease. (Anyone who has ever had a haircut knows that lack of communication can really produce a bad hair day). When I leave, my hair is always cut the way I want it. At Gregory's Barbershop, the brand promise is professionalism and consistency. It's not written down or displayed anywhere; it's just evident every time I get my hair cut. And I'm pretty sure that's why Gregory's customers keep coming back.

What is the brand promise you expose to your candidates? If you think job applicants aren't experiencing your brand promise, you're wrong. Are candidates treated with respect and dignity, or are they assaulted with paperwork, unneeded process and long waits in your lobby?

The manner in which you treat candidates is an expression of your brand promise.

What do your employees say about you as an employer? This is also part of your brand promise. If you don't know what your employees are saying, engage a company to conduct an employee survey. Be forewarned, however, about how people act when they are being observed or "probed." If you choose to hire a third party, be advised that employees often fear that honest "full disclosure" or "constructive criticism" will affect them negatively in some manner. Even the least paranoid people or Chatty Cathy in your organization will automatically think of "repercussions"—an ugly word. You'll need to reassure employees that their answers will be kept confidential by the survey firm, and your methodology should be carefully thought out so you can extract useful information in a non-threatening manner.

You also have to start thinking of referrals or "word of mouth," as they are sometimes unwittingly called. Word of mouth is, in reality, a totally different ballgame, as it has both negative and positive connotations. Referrals are completely positive, and they're what you really want. Attracting top performers to your organization works on a fairly accepted principle: Highly desirable candidates know other highly desirable candidates. You work hard to build and manage your reputation with prospective customers, so you must therefore build and manage your reputation with prospective hires. You want your people to refer other people to you, just as you hope your customers will refer other customers. Once again, you can see that you are constantly selling.

They say it takes a split-second to make a decision and a lifetime to stay committed to it. This means execution is the key to maintaining a brand promise. Just like mission statements that hang on a wall, a brand promise can be either useless words on a worthless piece of paper or a living embodiment of why your company is—and will continue to be—the best place to work in your market (or, if you're really shooting for the top, *anywhere*).

Develop your brand promise by once again looking at your differentiators. For instance, if one of your differentiators is "flexibility," you can embody this in your screening process by allowing candidates to interview after normal business hours (when babysitting may be easier) or to meet offsite—possibly even at their homes if you feel this can be accommodated safely and efficiently.

You get the point. You must get creative because, in the eyes of the candidate, this stuff matters and if everyone is reading books like this one, then everyone else is out there trying to be creative. The great ideas you have today can be played out tomorrow.

Your brand promise defines you, often before you define it, and you can either try to re-create it now (very difficult, but possible) or leverage what you have already.

Yes, I will use the same words again: This differentiates you from the clutter in the market. Building a pipeline of future stars is worth the effort. Use the brand promise exercise on the following page to get the process started

Figure 9-4

Brand Promise Exercise

How would you describe your organization's value to its employees? (Example: Consider GE's employee value to be global experience and world-class management development.)

Ask your top performers to describe the top three factors that drove their decision to work for your company.

1.)

2.)

3.)

Are the answers provided by your top performers similar to the details contained in your description? If so, you have your brand promise. If not, attempt to reconcile the differences by further exploring the answers provided by your top performers.

Sample Employee Brand Promise:
GE: To provide world-class management development in a global workplace.

Success Profiles

Have you ever heard the expression, "If you've got it, flaunt it?" Well, it works in recruiting, as well as fashion/modeling. If you've got top performers, leverage them. Flaunt them like a new Italian sports car. Talking to someone in the trenches carries more weight than someone who seems to officially represent the company. When the top performer tells the candidate that this is the right place for him and he can succeed, the message is much more meaningful than if a recruiter or manager says the same thing. You are paid to say good things about the company; they are not.

Top performers can mitigate fear and stress with a heaping dose of reality. We will talk more about this in a later chapter on "Closing the Sale," but fear, stress and the reality of job-hunting wreak havoc on the hiring process. Candidates become unnerved during the screening process and slowly back out the door. Do you really want someone who is so unnerved that he has one foot out the door?

Top performers can help diminish your risk of losing a great candidate by showing that real people—people just like the candidate in question—do succeed in this company. Involving your rising stars in the hiring process sends a clear message that they are the role models, and you want everyone to know it. It is the ultimate compliment and a win-win situation for you.

The concept is pretty straightforward. Write a short biography about each of your top performers. Interview them, and have them answer a couple of questions like:

- Why did you decide to work here?
- What do you like most about working here?
- What are the keys to your success here?

Document their answers with a picture of the profiled person. Don't over-engineer this. It is meant to be simple and easy to execute. It is meant to tell the story of why and how people succeed in your organization. Don't let it read like some glorious retirement swansong piece contrived at a bar over a fifth of dime-store scotch. Make it real, and don't blow smoke. If need be, find yourself a good copywriter. Perhaps you have one in your company already. If not, out-source the job. Just get it done.

Once these profiles are complete, create flyers as part of the candidate marketing package (more on that in a minute). Also post them on your website's career section, and use them at trade shows and recruitment events. Leverage them as often as you can. They will prove to be potent storytellers for you and they can deliver a unique message. Take a look at the next page for some examples, but don't be limited by what you see. Use the stories to create an image that best suits your company, as well as its message.

Figure 10-4

Success Profile Overview

Ask your top performers to answer the following questions. Choose the most interesting and well-rounded respondents to include in the profiles. Samples of completed Success Profiles are included on the following pages.

1.) What was your background prior to joining XYZ Company (or embarking on this career)?

2.) What made you choose XYZ Company (or this career) over other possible choices?

3.) What have been the primary keys to your success?

4.) How has XYZ Company contributed to your success?

5.) What advice would you give to someone considering XYZ Company (or this career)?

Career Opportunity Sell Sheet

Have you ever looked at the career section of most websites? Do you feel a bit warm and fuzzy inside after you do? I highly doubt it. But if you do, please forward these sites to me because I've been looking for them a long time and don't have a running list. For some reason, most companies think these coveted pieces of web real estate are simply a place to list jobs (mostly out-of-date jobs, at that). But for many potential candidates, this is the first contact they have with your company. Would you ever dream of having the rest of your website look as sparse and obsolete? I'm going to answer this question for you and ask: "Then why would you do it here?"

As an employer, you have an opportunity to define, for each candidate, who *you* want to be.

Career opportunity sell sheets can accomplish this for you in a consistent manner. A career opportunity sell sheet is an overview of your company and hiring process. They are designed to sell the work opportunities at your company, without letting the message go astray and end up in that gray, fuzzy zone. They need not be elaborate; rather, outline what the candidate should expect from your organization. Remember:

Simplicity is genius. Think of how good copywriting and commercials can communicate so much in 30 seconds. Use the sell sheet to keep things clear.

Here's a good example of how to use sell sheets. One of our clients, Ma Cher, is in the custom fashion design business in Los Angeles, California. It's a very hip company that is highly selective about the type of people it hires. The career section on Ma Cher's website spells this out in detail. Not only does the sell sheet (in this case, the web version) provide an appealing overview of the company, but it also details exactly what candidates will go through if they decide to throw their hat in the ring. (See the screen shot on the next page). The net effect: Ma Cher is positioned as a highly competitive employer that understands exactly what it wants. It is an organization that only the best should consider. Think back to the velvet-rope analogy: A bit of exclusivity never hurts.

Ma Cher serves as an excellent example because the company can take what it has created on its website and easily adapt it to a printed version for use at recruitment events, trade shows or anywhere else candidates congregate. It's also a great example of simplicity. The company hasn't overdone it. It has simply delivered a well-conceived, potent message that gets Ma Cher what it wants, with its own edge. Look at the examples on the following pages, and use them as a model for your business.

Package the Product

Now that you've done an admirable amount of work in developing your message, you're probably eager to use it. But before you start to deliver it, you need to practice one more step in this phase of the process: the package. Again, simplicity/genius is the theme. Develop a collateral package that can be disseminated when the time is right. This package can include anything you want, but at a minimum, be sure to include the following:

Company Overview
Product Sell Sheets
Success Profiles
Career Opportunity Sell Sheet

Get creative with this. Do you have a company newsletter? Include the last few editions. Have some entertaining photos from past employee gatherings? Include them, too. Develop your own think tank, and decide what matters most to you about the company. Then answer the question, and make sure it is embodied in your package. The checklist on the next page will help you pull everything together.

Figure 11-4

Collateral Package Checklist ☑

Think of your collateral package in the same manner as sales literature. It will never make a sale for you; rather, it may serve as a reminder, as well as a statement of commitment and professionalism.

- ☐ Corporate Overview

- ☐ Success Profiles

- ☐ Brand Promise Overview

- ☐ IPC Profile Overview

- ☐ Recent Press Releases

- ☐ Recent Articles

- ☐ Recent Newsletters

- ☐ Product Overviews

Positioning the Product: Summary

Just as you demand professionalism and preparation from your salespeople, you must demand it of yourself and your hiring managers. The standard product positioning process that companies go through every day can be your guide. You do not have to reinvent this process, by any means. Begin by focusing on the larger concepts. Differentiate your business by asking your top performers what makes you special. Convert the differentiators into a succinct elevator pitch to ensure that you capitalize on every rapid-fire interaction with a potential candidate. Build your brand promise to project a consistent and desirable image for candidates who actively engage in the hiring process.

After you complete these conceptual elements, you must do something more with this information. Use your top performers to create a series of success profiles, and allow them to communicate your positioning for you. Integrate this message and positioning into your career opportunity sell sheets, and use this information as handouts and on your web site. Lastly, assemble all materials in a collateral package, and distribute it to everyone who has contact with potential candidates. This may include anyone in your company, as well as spouses, significant others, boyfriends/girlfriends, cousins, sisters and the like. I don't want to appear to be going overboard here, and I certainly do not want you to go overboard. But everyone is a potential ambassador for your company, and you are striving for the good connotation of "word of mouth." But should you give everyone in the company license to manage this process at the level at which it should be executed? No. You want people who are specially trained and positioned to do the hardcore work for you. Your sales reps would never be on the street without solid information, so why would your hiring managers?

Chapter 4
Prospecting

Chapter 4
Prospecting

Up to this point, this entire book has been written to outline a new, improved process for the ongoing and systematic recruitment of talent for your business. Let's step back for one moment and look at the way things are done today. If such a thing as a recruitment program actually exists, it typically resembles the following:

1. Job opening becomes available within the company, based on promotion or voluntary/involuntary turnover.
2. Hiring manager contacts HR/an outside recruiter or advertises the job.
3. Candidates who may be seeking work submit their resume or application.
4. Haphazard screening process proceeds and best candidates are hired.

Is this a good process? Hell, no. Is this an accepted process? Hell, yes. Your company is perfectly normal if this describes you, under the accepted definition of "normal."

This process drives people like me nuts. Where do you think the system breaks down: Steps one, two, three or four?

If you chose step three, you win a prize. The killer words in that step are "who may be seeking work." This critically flawed process, used by the vast majority of companies today, is based on luck. If you're a manager who lives and dies by your ability to hire top talent, you are risking your career by relying on happenstance and luck. The last time I checked, gambling is against most company policies.

Now that we're clear as to where we are going wrong (in simple terms), let's return to the sales analogy. The "normal" hiring process is akin to a sales rep waiting until the pipeline is clear and there's one prospect left to call before filling the funnel again. If this were your rep, you probably would try like mad to get this fool trained and, if that did not work quickly, you would fire the individual without losing a minute of sleep. It is a foolish way to manage and/or execute a sales process, yet somehow it is a commonly accepted practice in talent acquisition and management.

 Systematically and consistently hiring high-potential talent is all about building and maintaining a healthy pipeline.

Just as with sales, some prospects in the pipeline will materialize, and most won't. We need to focus on keeping the pipeline robust. Without a constant focus on prospecting, we have absolutely no chance of building a solid pipeline of talent, let alone maintaining it. The previous chapters were about preparation. This chapter is about attraction and our ability to prepare the message and get the word out in an efficient, effective and consistent manner.

Here is one last comment on the need for constant prospecting, and perhaps it is the most critical. Without a strong pipeline, it is impossible to maintain high standards in the people we choose to hire because we really don't have a choice. Look at any supermarket candy aisle, and you know there's no chance that someone will leave without finding what he wants. Why? Because the market has almost every possible candy selection on the planet! Believe me. It also works in the opposite direction. If you have impeccable standards and constantly put the word out the way you are taught here, you will create exclusivity (the velvet rope) and your pipeline will look like the great supermarket candy aisle.

Without raised standards, we hire anyone who outwardly seems to have the skills—and suddenly we're in a horrible downward spiral. Too many companies earn a reputation for being the employer of last choice. It's like beer. In college, people drink the crap because that's all they can afford, and they don't really have any standard other than to get drunk. This is like a company whose standards have fallen. You can avoid being one of them by focusing on the pipeline. Following the advice from this chapter and completing the associated exercises are the keys to avoiding the pitfalls into which others are stepping.

Campaign Strategy

"One-half of the advertising dollars you spend will be well-spent. The other half will be wasted. The challenge is in knowing which half is which, so you need to spend it all." Did you ever hear that saying before? Ask any marketing professional and he will tell you that the first rule of advertising is a diversified and balanced approach. Like stocks, any one medium may or may not work, so a diversified and balanced portfolio is the best approach.

Recruitment marketing follows the same principle. The message may be different, but marketing is marketing—whether you are promoting a good product or career opportunity. The same principles that determine success and failure apply: Don't rely on luck. You must use a number of methods and produce a multipronged attack. Unfortunately, you do not know which medium will reach the "right" candidate, so you have to be proactive and always stay on the hunt. You can be reactive later, when you start to gauge your success and failure rates based on returns. At that point, you still do not switch to being reactive, but find and implement better methods for hunting.

Similar to any other marketing program, tracking results is imperative to spending time and money wisely. Monitor where your candidates are coming from and their quality. Some advertising media may not produce great numbers, but the quality may exceed that of other outlets. Large volume does not say much about your success. Tracking will allow you to see these patterns and act on them. The tracking spreadsheet on the following page will help you get started.

Let's talk about how you start building a campaign to attract top performers. I've said this before, but now is the perfect time to beat the drum: I don't have all of the answers here. Use your team to brainstorm, strategize and get creative. Order a pizza one night and ask everyone to brainstorm the question: "Where are my next top performers?" Have some fun with this, and don't be afraid to take some chances. Just keep tracking the results to see if those chances are paying off. The return on your investment is really just one great hire. After that, you should have a repeatable process, and your return on investment will climb.

Figure 12-5

Results Tracking Worksheet

Place a hash mark in the appropriate column(s) as candidates are identified. Use the description column to make any special notes about a candidate or the sources used to identify him/her. Based on your organization's resources, you can be as detailed or brief as you deem appropriate. Any type of spreadsheet allows you to identify basic trends and patterns affecting your business.

	Ad	Online	PR	Referral	Reference	Guerilla	Corporation
January							
February							
March							
April							
May							
June							
July							
August							
September							
October							
November							
December							

Direct Advertising

Help-wanted advertising is perhaps the oldest tool in the kit and the most widely used. Many heralded the onset of job boards like monster.com and hotjobs.com to be the end of newspaper advertising. Maybe this is or isn't the case, but it doesn't matter. It is still in the same category of advertising.

The fact is, as inefficient as this method is or may seem it probably should be included in your marketing mix. If you are on the pessimistic side of the spectrum, I ask that you at least attempt to do it right. I am writing this chapter on a Tuesday, fresh off of a good read-through of the Sunday Help-Wanted section of my local paper. This section contains all the "don'ts" of marketing for *good* (dare I say *great*) people. If you need a body to fill a seat, fine. Otherwise, let's get serious about it, and stop blowing your money on wasted newspaper (or electronic job board) space.

Here is how you develop a top-notch advertisement:

1.) Your ad must include your position information. Remember the differentiators and Ideal Profile that you worked so hard to develop? Now's the time to use them. Put them front and center in all of your job advertising. Make sure you write in layman's terms, not your industry's techno-speak. Why? Because if you are truly hiring for talent, you may miss someone who has it, but is turned off by the jargon and moves on to someone else. For examples, the following pages include a few particularly good ads you may want to model.

2.) Focus on responsibilities, or areas applicants will be accountable for, rather than tasks. Candidates don't want to hear they will be filing medical records every day. They want to know they will be responsible for all office organization and efficiency. See the difference?

3.) If you are using some form of direct advertising, follow this rule: *Do not wait for a job opening to run an ad!* Got it? This is an advertising campaign, and you shouldn't wait for an opening to run an ad any more than you should wait for your sales pipeline to evaporate before running an ad. The ads should be focused on job categories that are mission-critical or those that require frequent recruiting. Figure out the bread-and-butter job categories (i.e., sales, customer service, call center, operations, etc.), and keep the ads running.

Let's change gears and move from advertising "how's" to the "where's." This question/topic is a bit harder to answer and may be very specific to your immediate area. Employment advertising is nearly as prevalent as its product counterpart. Think of product advertising, as in toothpaste, cars, beer, etc. You will be thinking about your employment advertising in much the same way. The problem is the hit-and-miss nature of employment advertising, ranging from the innovative/truly useful to the ridiculous/wasteful. Try a few options; then track and try again. Something you think may be ridiculous may end up being a bull's-eye, and something that seems completely practical may strike out. Again, think of the stock portfolio:

Diversify and you'll be better equipped to gauge where your money should be spent in the future.

Ask Top Performers

Before we get into the myriad advertising options available to employers, let me start with a very obvious point: Ask your top performers how they found you. For that matter, survey all current staff to find out how they found out about your company. The answer to this question will tell you a lot about the different sources people use and possibly point out specific job-related correlations. For example, perhaps all of your customer-service agents found you in the newspaper, yet all of your salespeople found you in trade journals, while the programmers found you at a job fair. Or, you may find that while top people come from numerous areas, bottom performers tend to come from one source. You may find the opposite is true, but you won't know until you ask. Either way, this gives you a terrific starting point.

One last thought on this topic. If you are not tracking this information for each new hire, please start immediately. I always find it interesting when even large companies have no idea where their hires originate. You would never allow this lack of data in the sales process (I hope). You would realize that without good tracking, you have no idea how to effectively utilize your limited resources. Recruitment advertising needs to be treated in the same manner. I am not saying this is revolutionary or that you have never thought of this; I'm saying that, for some reason, certain processes and protocols get swept under the rug. Somewhere along the line, people seem to forget how crucially important this is to your company. It is easy to get bogged down with other projects and find yourself in a staffing quagmire.

By the way, if you haven't picked up on the fact that one possible answer for many of the questions in this book is "ask your top performers," you may want to go back and re-read a little bit. Now, let's explore the different options.

Advertising Options

Newspapers

Newspaper ads are the oldest form of job-search marketing and perhaps the most inefficient. A 2001 survey conducted by the Society of Human Resource Management found that the average cost per hire for an average metro-market newspaper is $3,295. Compare that to Internet recruitment strategy at $377.

My advice is to forget newspaper advertising, unless you are focusing on a very specific skill set, at which point trade publications (not really newspapers) make a great deal of sense. I have no axe to grind with newspaper advertising per se; it is just very expensive, wildly inefficient, and the shelf life is miniscule. Earlier, I talked about the failed strategy of relying on luck in recruiting. In many respects, newspaper help-wanted advertising is the definition of luck. In most cases, you run an ad for a week—maybe two—and hope the "right" candidate reads the paper during that time.

In today's job market, there are remarkably few positions that can be effectively marketed via the newspaper. The only possible exception would be particularly low-end positions. Many potential candidates for low-paying positions still rely on newspapers for their job search. If you do hire for this type of position, you may want to stick with this approach. Since I actually feel a bit bad about initiating a wholesale indictment of newspaper help-wanted advertising, let me throw something in the ring for its defense. Many publications (particularly the largest companies, such as Hearst and Gannett) are launching their own online services and other innovative programs to augment their traditional print model. In many communities, specifically smaller markets, this can be a good source of advertising. They often place your ad in multiple sources (Internet, print, job fairs) for a packaged price. See what your local paper has to offer, but avoid strictly print ads for most professional positions. There are far more cost-effective ways to go about it.

If you choose to ignore everything I just said and go down this path, please place "display" rather than "in-column" advertising. Display advertising looks just like a traditional product print ad, except it advertises a job instead of a product. By contrast, in-column ads (sometimes called "line ads") use that ridiculous newspaper syntax people choose to save money. These ads are really just lines of type with a very brief description of the job (tasks). They basically defy every principle on which this book is based, as advertisers usually remove words (and often letters from words), leaving prospective candidates with only the most obscure skills-based job description.

Also note that newspaper advertising is based on a simple premise: "Have an opening? Run an ad." This is the reactive approach. (Remember our discussion of step three, in which I asked where we went wrong?) This approach does little, if anything, to build your pipeline of talent and is therefore not the way to go, unless you are really desperate for candidates and are willing to pay a lot for advertising. (And most people who pay "a lot" do so because they let themselves become desperate in the first place.)

Online

If the help-wanted section of a newspaper represents the past, online job searching represents the future (and present, for that matter). When I first started in the recruitment business nearly a decade ago, online job searching was limited to only scientific and high-tech jobs.

Boy, has that changed. Today, most professional or managerial candidates use this method as their primary job search tool. That's why you may want to think twice about using the newspaper.

 Online advertising can offer you something that newspapers can't, which is global coverage, 24/7.

Typically, you pay one price (usually around $400 per posting), and your ad remains online for thirty to sixty days, depending on the site. Want to change the ad? Go ahead. (Try that with a newspaper. Good luck!) Even better, you can generally include as much content in the ad as you like. This is the perfect medium when you want to focus on the Ideal Profile because it requires an explanation. In most cases, you can provide links so a candidate can get more information on your company. There are really not many ways in which online advertising will not prove to be the most cost-effective and valuable method of advertising.

Lastly, online advertising provides you with the ability to maintain a general ad all the time. As of this writing, monster.com (generally accepted as the largest of the online job sites) is charging $365 for a sixty day posting. This means keeping a presence on the site for an entire year would cost $2,190—less than a one-day ad in the help-wanted section of most metropolitan newspapers! As a tool for constant prospecting, online advertising must be a part of your mix. Notice I did not say "could be," "can be" or even "should be." It *must* be!

Generally, online advertising offers a few different listing options for job openings:

1.) General Job Boards
These can be a good choice for most non-specialized professional positions (sales, customer service, etc.). The best known among the boards are monster.com, careerbuilder.com and hotjobs.com. Most jobseekers surf them all, so any of them is probably a safe choice.

2.) Specialized Job Boards
These are an excellent choice for highly specialized positions,

such as IT, engineering, medical, etc. The volume of candidates will probably be lower than with general job boards, but the candidate quality will most likely be excellent. Conduct a survey of your staff in these positions to determine the best site for the job level, as well as their preferred online career sites.

3.) Local/Regional Job Boards

Many positions do not require a national or international reach, and a local or regional site will suffice. In this case, most regions of the country have a mini-version of the general job board concept. Often, these are offshoots of newspaper help-wanted sections that carry the same benefits (and cost structure) as the general job boards. If you're unfamiliar with the local/regional choices available to you, call your local chamber of commerce for assistance.

Online advertising represents the newest method of job-searching. As far as the advertising portion of your campaign is concerned, this is an option you must explore. Always keep in mind that this is not the only pipeline-building activity you will be doing. At the least, it fits the bill for the advertising portion of that activity.

Radio/TV

For many positions, radio and/or TV advertising can be a highly effective option. If you fail to advertise creatively, however, broadcast ads can be a very costly option. You may not have considered radio/TV before, but in certain situations it makes sense. Typically, such advertising is used when an employer needs to hire a large number of people.

For example, one of my clients used radio very effectively when he expanded his call center by twenty-five positions. While he had a pipeline, it was nowhere big enough to meet his needs, so radio was one tool he used to quickly build a pool. It worked well. He also asked his current staff which stations they listened to and ran ads on those stations. Candidates came out of the woodwork, and my client managed to fill all of his positions. This, however, was a very specific situation, and I would not recommend it for any reason except mass hiring.

There *is* one way this type of advertising can be of great benefit: as a pipeline builder.

If you currently use radio or TV (or newspapers, for that matter) for traditional image advertising, integrate your recruitment message at the end of the ad.

While you are still focusing on your product message, you are gaining a bit of leverage by mentioning that you are always seeking talented, high-potential people for your workforce. It is a bit unorthodox, but it can really help keep the pipeline stocked at no extra cost to you. (You are already paying for the ad.)

If you have ever walked into a business franchise, chances are you've seen this strategy in action. Read the napkin in a Subway restaurant and you'll see a one-sentence solicitation for franchise opportunities. You, too, can follow this long-accepted practice for your business.

Trade Publications

If you are recruiting highly specialized people from a wide geographical range, trade publications may be the option to consider. At present, there is probably a trade association for almost every conceivable occupation, and there is typically one that is the most read within the field (with numerous "also-rans"). The also-ran publications generally have a reputation for being somewhat useful, but don't garner much respect in the industry. The accepted trade publications reach a unique, highly targeted audience and can help you effectively build a pipeline, especially for jobs that are difficult, costly and time-consuming to fill.

One major caveat that bears mentioning here is that relocation will almost always be an issue because these publications typically reach a national audience. The binding factor for these people is industry, not geography. For many people, it is important to stay in the industry, not to stay in a certain location, so if you don't want to (or can't) pay relocation expenses, this may not work for you.

If you believe trade publications are for you, create an ad for pipeline purposes—not necessarily based on a current job opening. There are two reasons for this:

1.) The kind of talent you are likely trying to reach is looking for long-term choices that may take long-term planning. As such, you are better off building your pipeline with trade advertising rather than using it to fill a specific position. You should therefore focus more on the Ideal Profile rather than the position.

2.) The shelf life of these publications can be quite long because they are often used for reference purposes. If you have an ad for a current opening and a high-potential candidate reads it a year from now, his logical thought process will be, "Oh well, the job must be filled by now." If, however, the ad is more general, the candidate may contact you instead of tossing you out with the bathwater.

It is too difficult and lengthy to get into cost at this point because it is a time-sensitive issue, and costs can vary wildly among trade journals. It simply depends on the publication. Contact your trade journals of choice, ask for a current media kit and go from there.

Nontraditional Advertising

Here is where you must get really creative. The opportunities are limitless because nontraditional advertising can be placed in locations that make sense based on specific factors in your business. Let's revisit my commission-only, advertising sales client, who brainstormed possible locations to reach high-potential candidates. His target audience is candidates who want maximum flexibility, which often translates to people who want to stay at home with their children during non-school hours. The client used schools, doctors' offices, PTA meetings, churches, etc., to post ads for some of his positions. Some people think this appears too low-class or grassroots, or they fear it will resemble guerilla-style advertising—all of which may have a perceived negative impact on their image. Don't, however, close your mind to this creative possibility. Many of these locations have areas where notices can be posted, and you should use them. These ads may not bring in huge numbers of candidates, but the cost will be minimal. If there's anything worth remembering, it's that it takes only one perfect candidate to make the difference. Another nontraditional method is direct-mail advertising. Lists are generated for just about every demographic these days. If you look hard enough and are willing to pay, you may just find the perfect list. Many, in fact, can be acquired for free, but some of the more specific lists will run you a few dollars. The client I just mentioned may want to consider buying a list of individuals who subscribe to parenting magazines. He could send a letter to each name on the list to test the waters and see what kind of response he gets. If his effort works, he may use lists more frequently based on the position he wishes to fill or to build a pipeline.

Again, consider all possibilities. Your goals should focus on building the pipeline. I suggested this before, but I will again: Schedule a brainstorming session with some current employees to answer the question: "Where are high-potential candidates for the role of 'X' found?" Let the options flow, and discredit nothing until you investigate it. Have some fun with this, and realize that most attempts will flounder—but one or two nontraditional sources can eliminate the competition and redefine your business. If you're not doing this now, chances are your competition isn't doing it either. By using more creative sources, you break through the clutter.

Tie-Backs

I briefly mentioned this concept before, though I didn't call it a tie-back. It therefore should be explored more fully.

Tie-backs involve tying one type of advertisement to another. In this case, you would tie recruitment to your non-recruitment–based advertising. If you do any type of advertising for your business, there is no reason not to include the message that you are always looking for high-potential talent. This includes, but is not limited to, creating a link to a "Careers" section on your website—an easy response mechanism. The beauty of this option is that there is no additional cost. I am not going to suggest a success rate or proffer statistical figures, but know that tie-backs may yield a few great candidates.

There are numerous recruitment advertising options available to you, and it may be worthwhile to hire professional help. If you do, make sure you're an active part of the process. The best thing you can do is learn the process so you don't have to pay for it the second time around. For now, use the matrix on the following page to help you get started.

Figure 14-5

Advertising Matrix

This matrix will help you identify the best places to advertise your opportunities.

Media	Consider Using If ...	Drawback
Newspaper	*Your opportunities are primarily low-level (i.e., laborers).*	*Short shelf life, very expensive, declining readership.*
Online	*Hiring for professional, managerial and customer-service positions; also for positions requiring ongoing recruitment and global reach.*	*Once placed, ad remains in various online forms forever; high candidate flow, often unqualified.*
Radio/ TV	*Opportunity requires hiring en masse at a rapid pace (i.e., staffing new call center).*	*Expensive, shotgun-type approach leads to unqualified candidates; short shelf life.*
Trade Publications	*Opportunity requires specific, hard-to-find skills; community limits candidate fields.*	*Can be expensive; candidates often require relocation.*

Networking

Remember the elevator pitch we discussed earlier? Dust it off. You're going to use it now because networking is an underused skill that requires practice. Many people I know are very good at it, but for some reason, they would rather run over their toes with the car than network. In reality, networking doesn't have to be painful and, for better or worse, it is perhaps the most effective way to build the pipeline. If you have some great aversion to it, then perhaps you can set up an internal training program designed to help others network, as well. The farther you spread the professional responsibility and accountability for some of these tasks within your company, the farther your reach.

It all starts with the elevator pitch. When your sales reps attend events with potential customer prospects, you would never accept a fumbling description of the value your business can deliver. You should work a solid pitch into their heads with fervor. The same emphasis will determine your success in networking. If you have not done so yet, go back and rehearse—and re-rehearse—the elevator pitch as though you're a salesperson in your company, trying to sell one of your products. Switch your company with the actual product, and prospect with the same fervor.

Usually, when you mention the word "networking," a very specific image comes to mind (at least in my mind): a bunch of suit-clad men and women wandering around a room, introducing themselves to one another. If you add the complimentary cocktails and mindless small talk, the concept usually sparks a negative connotation in most people's minds. (It's like a business trip: the trip is rarely fun, and if it is, you probably haven't been on many business trips.) No wonder networking is so often feared and dreaded. Perhaps this scenario works only for certain personality types.

 There are two critical words to remember when networking: constant and consistent.

Consistent refers to the message and constant refers to its execution. To experience real results from any networking strategy, you must be constant in your efforts. Not any one person or single networking event will make the difference. Consider the dynamic that exists: You are asking someone to speak to you about possible employment. Moments ago, this person didn't know you existed, let alone had any desire to engage in such serious dialogue. There's a good chance he also won't remember you one minute after you walk away. It will take *many* contacts to get the message out, but with a constant effort, you will succeed.

Creativity, once again, is the key to success. You must build and maintain top-of-mind awareness for your target market— meaning that you always cut through the clutter.

Here are some networking options that I've seen work. Use them to spark your thinking, and add them to your brainstorming sessions.

Trade Shows

If your trade-show booth fails to include a recruitment message, you are missing the boat. Trade shows are a magnet for people who are considering job changes—even complete career changes. Have you ever met a biochemist with a law degree? I have. Leverage your recruitment message, find someone who can deliver it verbally (in person), and assign him to your booth. Every square inch of your booth is real estate. Use it to recruit.

Business Cards

Take out a business card and turn it over. It's probably blank real estate. Use the back of the card to disseminate your recruitment message.

Here's another creative idea. I have a client who is constantly recruiting customer-service reps. He ordered business cards with the following message printed on the back: "Your service was excellent, and my company needs people with your passion and ability to service customers. Contact me about career opportunities today." He would hand out the cards to waiters, flight attendants and anyone else who caught his attention. Print this message on the back of employee business cards, and pay a small referral bonus to anyone who helps the company hire someone with this technique.

Resume Farming

I once met a technology recruiter who knew exactly how to get the resumes he needed. He worked for a relatively unknown company and needed to recruit good software developers. He built and nurtured a relationship with his local Microsoft sales rep and asked if he could have any resumes that Microsoft couldn't use. The recruiter created a new and highly qualified avenue for himself. Who gets the resumes you need? It may be someone who competes for your talent, but doesn't compete with your product. As this book adjusts your thinking, you will begin to hire for talent, while most other companies are still hiring for skills. Use this competitive edge to gain access to more resumes. Build and nurture a relationship *today* with anyone who can provide such help.

These examples are all networking-related, but they by no means form an exhaustive list. Do your research, decide where your candidates are located and go find them. Keep it simple, and don't expect too much from any one source. The power is in the exponential effect that numerous sources, when combined, can deliver.

Since I come from a human-resources perspective, I would like to mention something important here. In my foreword, I discussed our country's litigious leanings, which means I must mention gender relations when networking. Make sure, at all costs, that your elevator pitch does not contain any lewd, discriminatory or connotative language, including innuendos. Also be careful when networking at an event where alcohol is served. And when setting up an event, be wary of inviting employees with past histories of blurring personal and professional lines. (Networking is not the way for your single employees to meet their future spouses.) All it takes is one misunderstanding, or a minor or blatant foul, and your message—and your company—can take a huge hit from which you may never recover.

References

At different points in this book, I told you I wasn't going to teach you anything revolutionary. *Hire, Fire and The Walking Dead* was written to discuss creative ways to execute consistently. This section on references is possibly the one exception. If used consistently (getting used to that word yet?), references can have powerful consequences on your ability to recruit top talent.

Conventional wisdom dictates that references are no longer useful in today's litigious hiring environment. I cannot complete a speaking engagement or workshop without someone telling me that they no longer check references because it is a "waste of time." I frequently serve on panels of "experts," including employment lawyers who advise the audience to stop checking references and focus more on background (criminal, credit, etc.) checks instead. While I am a huge fan of background checks and firmly believe they need to be conducted in all hiring processes, all of this conventional wisdom is about as helpful as most other conventional wisdom: a good setup for an excuse.

 References, when handled properly, will become your number one source of pipeline generation activity.

They may not produce big numbers, but they will produce quality. When I first started my career, I taught jobseekers how to access the "hidden job market". References can represent access to this *hidden candidate market.*" The concept is not profound and simply means that winners fly with winners. Top candidates want to impress potential employers with the quality of their contacts, while losers struggle to provide anyone to speak on their behalf. Success leaves clues you do not have to look for, and these clues are called "people"—people to whom you may speak. You should always check references and, when desired, turn these calls into recruitment calls. For every ten or so references checked, you will convert one or two into candidates, if done properly. The following paragraphs describe a reference process you may follow to execute consistently.

Your first step is to ask every candidate for five references. Do you usually ask for three? Why? You probably can't answer that question, can you? Most likely, it is because everyone else does this, so you follow suit. This book is about differentiation, right? Here is one of your many chances to initiate your differentiators. You are not looking for just any references. Be specific. You want a minimum of three professional peer references, which consist of people candidates work with in their current role. The other two can be supervisors or subordinates, whichever mix is appropriate in your case(s). You can change the mix to suit your needs, but make sure the predominant number suits your area of need.

Any references that do not suit your current recruiting needs can be turned over to HR for a check (if you do this currently). The remaining references must be checked by the hiring manager. Remember: These are recruitment leads and need to be dealt with in that respect, but from an actual reference point of view, the hiring manager should be the one to personally hear the information emanating from the reference. This includes the need to assess any "nuances" and "unspoken" areas of concern—in other words, any negative connotations that arise in the conversation.

And from your recruiting perspective, you can convert the final dialogue to a conversation regarding the reference himself. You can say something like, "Thank you for your time and information. Candidate A spoke very highly of you, and I can see why. What are you doing currently? Terrific. We are always looking for people like you and Candidate A, so if you are ever interested in discussing potential opportunities, I hope you will call me."

Send a handwritten thank-you note, accompanied by your business card and a reminder that you are always looking for talented, high-potential people. Ask the source to contact you if he/she would like to discuss employment possibilities. Then add the reference to your candidate database for periodic contact.

This doesn't sound too tough, does it? It can be incredibly powerful if used consistently and correctly, but here's one word of caution: Every so often, I encounter a workshop participant or audience member who becomes a bit overzealous and forgets one critical component of the call—to check the reference! Let me be very clear: I am in no way minimizing the importance of the reference-checking process itself. The entire next section is all about how hardcore diligence is the bedrock upon which this entire process rests. Rather, this is about leveraging the reference to assist in the pipeline-building process. You must check the reference—and check it well. If the individual with whom you are speaking seems like a high-potential candidate, great. If not, complete the reference and move on. If you do not take the reference part of the call seriously, it will look like a scam, and your credibility—as well as your company's—will be severely damaged in the process. Not to mention, you could end up losing the candidate whose references you were checking in the first place.

Referrals

Referrals can be another great source of job applicants if they are handled with some TLC. Many companies have some kind of employee referral bonus program in place, which usually results in mixed results. If you do not have a program like this, start one today. It is not hard to initiate or administer, so there is no excuse for failure to implement one.

Let's go a bit beyond the typical employee referral programs and look at other best practices that have delivered results. Some are quick and easy while others require more time and resources. It depends on what works for you and how aggressive you must be to reach your recruitment targets.

Ask any decent sales professional and they will tell you that to really maximize referrals, you must manage a system of referral generation. In a nutshell, this means identifying the proper time to ask— and the manner in which you will ask—for a referral. Unfortunately, the minute I mention "referral" to most people, tensions immediately begin to rise. Non-salespeople seem to have vivid flashbacks to the bad sales rep who handed them a card and asked them to fill in three names, while delivering the worst and least sincere plea. This plea usually rested on the claim that his business was based solely on referrals. Guess what? Everyone's business is based on referrals. It just so happens that most people deliver the request more honestly and tactfully.

The best place to begin the referral-generation process is with brand-new hires. They want to impress you at this point, so leverage their eagerness, and ask both early and often. As soon as the candidate accepts employment with your firm, begin the referral-generation process. Explain to each new hire that you are building a world-class team and believe he/she is a world-class performer. Serious performers like him/her usually know other people who would make good coworkers. It may take a couple of conversations, but keep it up and it will pay off. This is a perfect opportunity for new hires to make a good impression.

I recently held a workshop in which a participant suggested an innovative approach: exit interviews. During the exit interview, you should ask the exiting employee to recommend either a replacement or someone who may be a good fit for another position in your company. Of course, there is the blinding glimpse of the obvious here: You should do this only when an employee is leaving on good terms.

Since we are talking about getting referrals at all stages of the employee life cycle, let's try one more stage: to elicit a referral from an employee who has already left your company. One can hope that when people leave your company, their parting feelings are positive. If this is true, forming an alumni club is a terrific way to capture this goodwill and leverage it for future recruitment. The biggest consulting and professional-services firms often use this strategy, but it can work for any company, large or small. The approach can also vary from complex and expensive to cheap and easy.

In case you are unfamiliar with this concept, a company alumni club is exactly the same as, or similar to, a college's or university's. You are providing an outlet for people who once worked together to reunite, socialize and network. From a recruitment standpoint, this can pay tremendous dividends. You are providing a valuable service to these individuals, who often want to remain in contact with one another, and it continues to build goodwill in your company. Best of all, it is a great way to generate solid, top-performer referrals.

There are two ways your recruitment efforts can benefit from an alumni club:

1.) The alumni may actually consider returning. It is not uncommon for an employee to work at a single organization several different times throughout his career. Sometimes a key piece of experience he needs to build his resume cannot be gained in your company. He must obtain it elsewhere, feel satisfied or secure, and come back to your company at a later date. When good people leave (the best will leave faster than anyone else), keep them close. Maintain and build upon the relationship you have fostered throughout their employment with you. An alumni club is a great way to do this.

2.) Alumni who feel good about you as their past employer are very willing to refer others to your company. Like all of us, these people lead busy lives. If you are not proactive, they will not stop to think of referring someone to you. The alumni-club strategy ensures you are in their thoughts and continue to play an active part in their lives. Marketers call this type of approach "top-of-mind awareness," which I cited earlier. Call it whatever you like, but I highly suggest you do it because it works.

Now you know "why" you need to try this, so let's switch gears and talk about "how" you do it. The answer really depends on your company. If you own a large company with alumni spread out all over the country or world, a more deliberate strategy is necessary. If you own a small company with alumni residing nearby, a quarterly get-together at a local bar, with chicken wings and beer, may be just the ticket. The following approaches may work for you. When you launch an alumni club, remember:

1.) Don't overdo it or make it overly complex to administer. I have seen companies go wild with this concept, only to have it fail soon afterward because no one had the time to drive it forward. The monster became too big and hairy, and the benefit was lost. When I mentioned being aggressive, I did not mean pushy. "Top-of-mind" means you cannot ignore something, while "pushy" means the expectations are too high and there is a feeling of obligation that's being forced upon someone. Did you ever have a college alumni officer who needed to "get a life"—the one who gave you attitude about not showing up at functions or seemed to note every time you were late or left early? The key is to manage expectations on both sides to ensure everyone is benefiting.

2.) You must provide some value to the alumni. No one wants to take time away from their families and friends to attend an event that carries no benefit. Focus your content around areas of value. How about a session on career planning? Consider booking a networking expert to help members build their Rolodexes. Or how about a work/life balance expert? These are relevant topics to anyone in the work world, and they usually entice people to show up.

3.) Make someone in your organization accountable for the continuation and success of the program. Someone must feed the program, love it and keep it alive. Using any of the tools in this book, you can clearly identify this employee and add it to their job description (after some negotiation). If you feel as though everyone is already overloaded, add club administration to a relevant open position's job description, and include this detail in your job search. Do you already have an office manager who is great at planning events and looking to take on more responsibilities? Terrific! You've got the person.

Other Referral Sources

Referrals are available everywhere you go, provided you're not afraid to ask. Think about all of the people you deal with on a daily basis. They can help you build your pipeline. What about customers? Are you asking them to help you? Again, this is a potential referral chain that is highly relevant to your success. The more successful you are in helping current customers, the more willing they'll be to give you referrals. In turn, you will become more successful. People love to help people who help them.

How about vendors? Talk about a group that's motivated to help you and impress you! Smart vendors make value-added services a top priority. Referrals of high-potential candidates are the biggest value they can provide to your business. Start by asking them and continue to ask. Of course, this is contingent upon the vendor liking you. Every time I discuss this vendor-referral idea, I always think about a former client: one of the best-known companies in the world. When you visit the office, you see a beautiful plaque hanging over the main reception desk, which eloquently explains that all visitors represent an extension of the company and help define how it is viewed. And since these visitors—including customers, vendors or other guests—are so important, they are to be treated with respect and care.

Unfortunately, these words were all talk. It was obvious, as soon as you walked beyond the plaque and into management's offices, that vendor-crushing was a sport that defined an employee's success in this company. Clients were routinely advised that it was a privilege to do business with this company. If this meant you took a loss, then so be it. On top of that, payment terms were stretched over 100 days. If payment was made prior to that, the company would take a discount for prompt payment. Needless to say, very few vendors were referring future candidates to this company.

I share this story as a reminder. People will not refer others to your company if there is any question as to how they will be treated. If you are having problems getting candidate referrals, look not only at who and how you are asking, but at your outside image, as well. Would *you* refer friends to your company? If the answer comes with any hesitation, fix this problem first. Surveys are a good way to unmask your reputation in the job-applicant community. When conducted properly, surveys can be a tremendous tool for problem identification. Use an outside service so responses will be honest and employees won't fear reprisal.

If you really think through your approach, there are limitless ways to generate candidate referrals. And if you happened to notice, I never once suggested that you ask anyone to write three names on an index card. Can you imagine that?

Public Relations

We all have a story to tell. One story you should be telling is how your company contributes something constructive and meaningful to society, including good jobs. Get the word out.

One of my greatest learning experiences occurred during my first job, fresh out of college. I was doing PR for a major Boston agency with a blue-chip clientele. The profound lesson I learned was that when information is presented in an interesting way, the media will run with just about anything. Editors have space that needs to be filled, and you can help them fill it. I am not trashing newspaper or magazine editors and writers, but this is akin to having someone complete your English homework for you legally throughout college. Just make a couple of corrections, add a few of your own buzz-words, change the title, and voila!

Armed with this lesson, I used it with great success when I started my first company. We needed people—very talented people—and we needed them badly. We were completely unknown in our community and industry, both as a company and as individuals. Needless to say, no one was looking to us for employment, and no one was eager to help us. But as I stated earlier, people love to help people who help them. To cut through the community clutter, we focused on making ourselves interesting—or, at least, "loud." Press releases rolled out every time anything happened in the company. Getting new customers was one motivating factor, but getting candidates to recognize us was the bigger piece of that pie. Make a note: PR made this happen.

Have you landed a new client? Send a press release to the media. Have you hired someone new? Send a press release with a biography and a picture to your local business press. Has your office moved? Send a release highlighting your need for larger space to accommodate your fast growth. Anything, if spun right, can be of interest to the media. Admittedly, this does require an eye for promotion, so find someone within your company who has a talent for this kind of work. Salespeople or marketing people usually have a knack for PR. If you are struggling to find someone internally, then you may need to hire an outside PR agency. Just make sure they understand that recruitment is one area you will partly define by the agency's success. It is not solely about product sales (though that is critical, too).

Let me jump back to one idea I have already mentioned because you don't need a PR agency to do this. Whenever you hire or promote a new person in any kind of professional or managerial role, create a press release (example on next page). It is not difficult; you just need a quick release that mentions the name and new position, along with the individual's biography and photo. Most business newspapers have a section that runs this type of story anyway, so don't feel as though you are pushing useless information onto their desk. By doing this consistently, you will develop a reputation as a company that has a lot going on and one that values the press and its prestige in your community.

With my local paper, I am always amazed at how effectively this strategy is used by some companies. There are handfuls of companies that appear in the paper almost every day (or at least it seems like this is the case). As with the alumni-club approach, accountability is the key to success here.

Have one person in your company who is accountable for compiling the promotions/hiring announcements and sending them to the appropriate media.

In my last company, this was our office manager. In your company, it may be HR. No matter—just make sure someone is accountable for getting it done consistently and effectively.

Let me change gears for a moment and offer another way to use the hiring-announcements section of your business press. First, be sure to read these announcements regularly. They are leads. If you see someone hired or promoted by another company, consider the individual a potential for your pipeline. Drop the person a note. One very effective way to initiate contact is to clip the announcement and include it with your note, congratulating the person and explaining that you are always looking for high-potential people. Let these up-and-comers know that, if they ever feel the need to discuss other opportunities, they should call you. You will get calls. Statistically, about one in three people is either actively engaged in, or has considered, a job search. This means that for every three notes with clips that you send out, one will resonate. I don't know about you, but I like those odds.

Take a look at the PR samples on the following pages, and get started today. It's only difficult if you overcomplicate it, so bite off one or two ideas that work for you, and do them over and over again.

Headhunters

I am a headhunter (and now so are you), but not in the classic sense. The field of headhunting is about the least understood and most disrespected of any I know, and for good reason. Bluntly, the vast majority of headhunters are terrible, and they call negative attention to themselves and the field. Many will charge you exorbitant rates and then deliver little more than a resume when you are at your most desperate hour. They have had devastating consequences, not only on people's bottom lines, but on the industry as a whole.

The truth is that a great headhunter or recruiting firm can be as valuable to your company as a superb accountant or lawyer. If you find one, make him part of your professional-services team. The challenge is to wade through the muck to find the truly valuable ones. A skilled headhunting firm uses many of the tactics that I have discussed in this book, as well as others I lack the space to cover. These experts are your eyes and ears on the street and can proactively deliver excellent candidates to your doorstep.

So, how do you know the difference? Here's what to look for:

1.) Specialty
Does the firm have specialized niches, or will it take any assignment that comes along? Work with the specialty recruiters because, more often than not, they will intuitively understand your needs. Specialties come in all shapes and sizes. Some specialize in job categories (sales, engineering, etc), levels (executive, entry, etc.) or industries (construction, airline, etc.). Some will say they have a specialty, but what they really have is a lack of clients. They are merely pigeonholed because they stink. Ask for multiple references from the firm, and check them thoroughly (just as you would check an employee's references). Armed with this book, you should have no difficulty in checking references. Just remember: If they are truly specialized, they will have no problem providing proof.

2.) Methodology
Where are candidates coming from? Many of the truly awful

people in this field recruit solely from the big online job boards. You give them a position to fill, and they instinctively go to monster.com and locate some candidates. After speaking briefly to them, they forward certain candidates for your consideration. This is not worth $20,000, if you ask me. Too often, a client's low standards allow them to get away with this approach. Check your contract, and if it doesn't suit you, ask to provide new provisions to define success and payment. Ask them to describe their candidate identification and screening approach. It should entail involvement from your company, at some level. If they struggle with an answer, move on fast. Ask to speak to some candidates who have been placed by them, and ask those people how they were screened. I assure you that the truth will quickly unfold before you.

3.) Longevity
How long have they been in business? While this is by no means a hard rule, recruitment firms tend to come and go fast. They burn through a handful of clients, and they're finished. Find out how long their recruiters have been with the company, and make sure you verify any/all information with the actual person.

4.) Retainer Versus Contingency
Recruitment firms typically use a retained search-fee structure (you make a partial payment up front, and you're billed throughout the process) or contingency fee structure (they get paid if and when you hire one of their candidates). I am not a fan of contingency searches because it usually means there is a poor screening process. With contingency fees, the recruitment firm wants to get the candidate to you as fast as possible, and it usually sells you hard on the candidate. It clearly is not on your side because it needs you to hire someone, whether the candidate is good or bad, before it makes any money. Retained firms are squarely on your side and have the luxury and time to identify the best candidates. They carry more risk to you, but it's worth it.

If all of this sounds like a lot to remember, use the recruitment firm screening tool to help you get started.

Figure 16-5

Recruitment Firm Screening Sheet

Use these questions to identify the right recruiting firm for your needs.

1.) What is the firm's specialty?

2.) How many placements have been made within this specialty in the last 12 months? How many outside the specialty?

3.) Are references available from clients who successfully hired employees within this specialty? If so, request a minimum of three.

4.) Are references available from candidates who were placed within this specialty? If so, request a minimum of three. Ask the references about the firm's expertise in the specialty area, as well as screening methodology. How was the candidate sourced?

5.) How long has the firm been in business? Assess the professional backgrounds of its partners and recruitment staff. (Note: If the firm is new, this is not a disqualifier; rather, fall back on the background of partners and staff.)

6.) Is the firm contingency- or retainer-based? What are the payment terms and guarantees?

Ongoing Marketing

One bad day—this is what it's all about. You've built your pipeline, and you now wait for a candidate to have one bad day at his current job. Whenever I think of the best hire I made, one name always comes to mind: Jeff. He was clearly a strong, steady performer in every respect, starting as a recruiter for me and eventually advancing to junior partner. It took us nearly two years to land Jeff, and this is what this section is all about: waiting. One day, Jeff had a bad day at his current job and said, "Enough!" We had built and nurtured the relationship for two years, and we were ready for his call. It just took a lot longer than most people would wait.

The first meeting we had with Jeff was at a trade show. He impressed a couple of partners in the company, and they invited him to lunch. They started the twenty month pursuit. Anyone with a little bit of savvy can identify a high-potential candidate, but few have the discipline to stay with it. An ongoing marketing program can help you do this systematically.

Consider your sales process for a moment. A sales rep goes to meet a prospective customer and, while they are a good prospect, the timing to move the deal forward is not right. What do you tell your reps to do in this familiar case? One hopes there are many answers to this question. Perhaps you have a newsletter that is periodically sent to all customers and prospects. Maybe the rep visits with or calls the prospect every few months.

 There are many ways to maintain top-of-mind awareness. Maintaining your recruiting pipeline is no different.

To do this effectively, you must have some system to collect and house the candidate pipeline data. If you own a larger company, chances are this is accomplished through an applicant tracking system. If you own a smaller company, a simple Excel spreadsheet can be the answer. The bottom line: House the data in an organized, user-friendly fashion.

I tell our salespeople to put the prospect "on a program." By this, I mean they should design a follow-up strategy based on the needs of

the individual contact. Contact points should be staggered to minimize intrusiveness, while maximizing contact. Ever had sales reps
who would not go away? Their follow-up method consisted of constant calls, in which they acted like your best friend? This is not
what I'm talking about. This just shows a serious lack of training,
creativity and professionalism. Incidentally, if you have a sales manager who allows this behavior, have him trained or get him a new job
(with another company).

No matter what a candidate in your pipeline thinks of you, he probably doesn't want to hear from you every week. So, use your tools.
Do you have a company newsletter? Get him on the mailing list. This
is a less intrusive touch-point than a useless phone call. Sending out
a press release? Send it to your candidate pipeline, as well. It keeps
prospective employees in the loop and proves that exciting things are
happening at your company. Do you have an interesting story about
a candidate's field? Send it to him. Limit the phone calls to once
every couple of months, unless you believe the candidate is getting
ready to jump soon.

Let's go back to Jeff's story. After that initial lunch meeting, we used
all of these tools. I, or another partner, would call him every two to
three months, but we were not limited to this approach. We created
and designed a program built around our expected timeframe for
him, and we knew this timeframe would be long. And when Jeff was
finally ready to move, it was a natural transition to our company.
We had been engaged in a dialogue for such a long time that he
already knew he would be highly valued. Do you honestly think his
choice was difficult? (P.S.: I have never told Jeff this story before,
so he is reading it here for the first time. Thank you for a great and
worthwhile story, my friend.)

Prospecting: Summary

You would never allow a sales rep to forget about building his
pipeline until he desperately needed the next sale. Why would you
do so for recruitment? Prospecting allows you to build and maintain
a healthy, vibrant pipeline of talent. But to build this pipeline successfully, you must employ a campaign strategy that consists of many
elements. This will create a magnifying effect on your pipeline over

time. This campaign can use many traditional marketing tools, such as newspaper, online, radio/TV and trade publication advertising, as well as many nontraditional "guerilla-style" tactics.

Additionally, your prospecting strategy must include other techniques, such as networking, referrals, PR and headhunters. The most powerful of these strategies is reference-checking. Always remember:

To maintain the health of the pipeline, you must creatively sample ongoing marketing extensions (up-and-coming or fresh) to keep top-of-mind awareness among your candidates.

Whichever tools and techniques you use, your pipeline will be the lifeblood of your recruitment efforts' ability to move forward.

Chapter 5
Qualify

Chapter 5
Qualify

"Engineering logic"

These are the words a highly regarded CEO friend uses when describing how hiring decisions should be made. If you have anything in common with me, you may not possess any logic that could be compared to an engineer's. Either way, though, the concept is as profound as it is simple. An engineer uses as many data points as possible before drawing any final determination. Multiple data points are the core of good due diligence. For example, candidate qualification "data points" may include prescreen, test, behavioral interview, reference checks, background checks, etc. But here is the key to engineering logic: A significant gap in any of these areas will cause the bridge to fall. Start over and rebuild. Now that you have a pipeline, you can be choosy.

By now, I hope you have recognized the importance of keeping the candidate pipeline stocked. Like any perishable commodity, it becomes rotten over time and needs to be continually refreshed to guarantee success. A lot of opportunities will enter the pipeline— some great, some fair—and sometimes you just can't figure out how they got there in the first place. Success, in no small measure, is determined by your ability to separate the good from the bad and focus your time where the chances of a match are greatest. This is what qualification is all about.

Any true sales professional will tell you that their ability to produce results is determined by how well he focuses on people and the activities that make him—and, subsequently, his company—money. He will also tell you that not all business is good business. You can close the deal, only to regret it later. These are the deals that you sensed in your belly were bad, but didn't want to admit it and we generally respond by wanting to "fire" the clients.

This is particularly true in the recruitment process. Pipeline building is critical for one reason and one reason only: When you need people the most in your company, you can still be particular with the type of person you hire. If you think about the poor hires you have made, I'd bet the majority of them were the result of a "desperation hire." Perhaps a key person quit unexpectedly in your busy season, and you therefore responded in the only way that made sense: You took the best candidate in front of you at the time and said, "To heck with the consequences." What else could be expected of you in this situation? It's only natural, and a business necessity demanded it. That is precisely why having the pipeline is critical. It saves you from other "business necessities" that are bad for business.

Without the pipeline in place, you have few, if any, candidates from which to choose. Having fewer candidates means you will need to lower your standards and overlook many negatives, focusing on gray-area or Hail-Mary positives (whatever you can dig up) and get them into the seat. These scenarios are all too common, and they are not going away. They are a business reality, and we must stop being surprised by it and start dealing with this reality proactively. The pipeline is the cure.

Ask any sales manager what struggling reps do when their back is against the wall. You will hear that they take any business they can find. This bad business creates unhappy customers (your solution wasn't the right one for them from the start), and unhappy customers diminish your reputation, thus making it harder to sell in the future. The cycle continues its downward spiral for the struggling rep until they ultimately leave. It's not a giant leap to equate this to the recruitment process.

Your ability to have a robust pipeline of candidates from which to qualify is the key.

 Candidate qualification is the process by which we go about taking passive candidates and assessing whether they will fit in our company.

To have your recruitment or screening process meet the criteria for adequate due diligence, you will need to include proper steps, such as behavioral interviewing, testing, reference checking and background checking. I say "adequate" for a reason. While "adequate due diligence" is an oxymoron, many companies have appallingly low standards for candidate qualification, yet believe their methods constitute due diligence. Their definition of the screening process consists of a totally unprepared and untrained staff member asking a few questions. They convince themselves they have a good "gut feeling" for people.

Unfortunately, gut feelings in the hiring process are about as bad an indicator as throwing a dart to make your decisions. Actually, they may be worse because interviewing is a skill. You may be lucky when throwing the dart because the skill is actually directed. Many candidates know exactly how to handle an interview, and if you are not properly prepared, or you lack a strategy and/or training, you have no way of dealing with this. This section is all about giving you the tools to combat candidates' interview skills and to separate the good from the bad. Casting aside even mediocre candidates won't be a challenge for you once you have confidence in your pipeline.

It's a Human Game

Professionally, few things irritate me more than hearing people say that hiring is a numbers game. This is absolute nonsense, and you should avoid those who say it like the plague. At its very essence, hiring is a human game. We are dealing with human beings who have families to support, reputations to uphold and standards to maintain. Some companies select candidates on a provisional basis and, if the candidate fails, the company figures there are plenty more where they came from. This attitude is one reason for the breakdown in company loyalty that is so prevalent today.

This is not only a morally vacant mindset, but it is bad business, as well. Disgruntled employees are worse than unhappy customers. They take it more personally and dream about your failure. Are you going to get it right every time? Probably not. But if you start with a well-built strategy, you will greatly increase your chance of succeeding. Now that I'm off my moral soapbox and done with the platitudes, let's take a look at how we can qualify candidates for maximum success.

Fit to Ideal Profile

Remember the Ideal Profile concept I introduced in Chapter 2? Now is the time to really put it to work for you. The Ideal Profile is going to be the measuring stick used to select the best candidates. If you recall, this profile is based on the qualifications and characteristics of our top performers.

First, let me remind you what characteristics we used to develop the Ideal Profile: intellect, personality, cultural fit and hard skills. While this is an easy enough concept to understand, it can be a bit tricky to assess. The only real answer is a multipronged attack. This chapter will cover the elements of the attack and how to use them systematically.

Application

Without question, the employment application is the most over-looked and underutilized form of screening. Generally, companies order generic application forms from their local office-supply store and ask candidates to complete them, file them and forget them. But when used correctly, applications can be a highly effective tool for early-stage prescreening.

An application can ask low-value, but important, questions that can immediately disqualify a candidate with poor potential.

It can also allow a candidate to opt out for many integrity issues. For example, one client uses an application that requires a candidate to sign a waiver for an intrusive reference check. The end result, when combined with waivers for background checks, is a voluntary opt-out by candidates with something to hide.

An application also allows you to look for discrepancies. I am still shocked at how often references and resume details fail to jibe. Comparing the two is an easy way to test for integrity (and maybe intelligence). Applications should be an important part of your over-all qualification process. Leverage them to give yourself time, weed out low-potential candidates and add another valuable data point.

Lastly, you can take the application well beyond the typical questions. One of the field innovators that is truly accelerating the process of recruitment through the thoughtful use of applications (as well as very unique candidate sourcing) is Accolo (www.accolo.com). This company is a great example of what is possible, utilizing advanced technology in the recruitment process.

Prescreen

Screening candidates can be time-consuming. There are ways to pre-screen that force candidates to do some of the work for you. If you think about your screening process, there are probably a few deal-killer questions that you consistently ask. Depending on the position, they may be as simple as "Do you have a high school education?" or as complex as "Explain your experience with white-light LED technology in Mandarin Chinese." (This was an actual question from a search I once worked on—I swear.) Anyway, prepare these questions ahead of time and give them to the candidate after you have received his resume. Have him answer the questions and send them back to you.

This very simple technique will save you and the candidate the time and aggravation of dealing with a face-to-face interview for a low-potential hire. Depending on the position, some of these questions also may be deal-breakers and low-value questions at the same time. This also sounds like an oxymoron, but it's not. Dealing with low-value questions in the prescreen helps you avoid wasting time during the interview. Think of each interview question as a guidepost in your decision, and make each one count.

A workshop participant on the West Coast once told me a story about a candidate from the East Coast. He looked at this candidate's resume, and it was stellar. Next, he conducted an interview over the phone, and it went very well. Finally, he flew the candidate in for a personal interview. During the interview, after all of the money and time had been spent, relocation became an immediate issue. The candidate falsely believed that working from a remote location was possible. This is why it's important to figure out your baseline requirements and provide them to the candidate in advance. You will be amazed at what you will find out. You will also be pleasantly stunned by how much it will free you up to focus on the high-value screening areas. Remember that high-value issues are those you identified in your Ideal Profile. Though it may be a must for someone to relocate, it does gauge whether he can do the job or is appropriate for it.

Figure 17-6

Sample Prescreening

Prescreening questions should be low-value, nonstarter types of queries that allow you to get to the heart of the screening process more rapidly. Here are some sample questions.

1.) Are you willing and able to relocate?

2.) Can you lift 50 lbs.?

3.) What are your salary requirements?

4.) Are you willing and able to work for 100% commission?

5.) Are you legally permitted to work in (country name)?

6.) Have you ever been convicted of a felony?

7.) Do you have a clean driver's license?

8.) Do you possess a (name the license) to work in our industry?

9.) Are you over the age of 18?

Testing and Assessment

If you are not doing any testing and assessment, you are missing one of the most effective, high-quality forms of candidate screening available. Obviously, I'm a big believer. Subjectivity is the real killer in the qualification process. So many extraneous factors can influence our ability to interview effectively. The smell of perfume or cologne, the color of a suit, an accent and countless other things create associations for us, both positive and negative. Have you ever interviewed a candidate during a very bad day at the office? How would you like to be that candidate? It can also work in the other direction. On a day when you closed the deal of a lifetime, your defenses are down, and any candidate looks like a dream. Employment testing can be the fulcrum that keeps us centered. While I would never suggest that it be the sole basis for making hiring decisions, it should play a major influential role.

For those who have used some form of test battery in the past, an image usually comes to mind. For decades, testing was the domain of the industrial psychologist. A company would ask a candidate to take a written exam. After completing the questionnaire, it was sent to the I/O Psychologist for scoring. A lengthy report came back a few days later containing a bunch of big words that you did not understand. You picked up the phone and said, "Listen, Doctor. Bottom line. Should I hire this person or not?" At this point, you got the answer you were seeking.

That was then, this is now. Current assessment technology is fully automated and delivered online. It measures multiple dimensions of the candidate, including the intellectual, personality and cultural fit for the job. Recommendations are given to fit a profile of people who are doing the job for you today (i.e., your top performers). The tools also consist of gap analyses that dynamically generate interview questions, coaching tools and development suggestions for the candidate, if you are to hire him. Even better, candidates can take the test from home.

Why am I impressed with this technology? It takes so much of the "gut feeling" out of the hiring process. When used at the beginning of the screening process, it helps remove low-potential candidates, while freeing us to fully explore the high potentials. It does so based on comparative data held within our company today, thereby removing much of the subjectivity from the screening process. You are matching the current candidate with a company profile created by looking at your current top performers.

One of the best practices regarding the use of any testing product is to use it as early in the screening process as possible.

I strongly urge you to do so immediately after the prescreening and before you start conducting personal interviews. You want to eliminate the low-potential candidates early on, before your subjectivity and so-called gut feelings begin to take hold and permanently taint the search. When candidates reach your desk for further interviewing, they should be solid, qualified and potentially successful. After they have taken the assessment, we will use this information to further our interviewing process.

There are a couple of critical considerations when embarking on a testing program within your company. First, choose the right assessment for your needs. The testing market has many options from which to choose. To determine the right test for you, answer two vital questions:

1.) What positions will I be testing for?
2.) What is the driving business need?

The first question is most important. Why do you want to test at all? There are many reasons that can drive the business need—for example, high turnover, low productivity or theft. These are just a few examples among hundreds. The answer to this question will help you choose the solution for your specific needs. On the next page, you'll find a matrix to help you make decisions.

	Executive/ Managerial	Customer Facing/ Professional	Labor
Turnover	Cognitive, Behavioral, Cultural (CBC) Assignment	CBC & Skills	Skills & Integrity
Productivity/ Quality	CBC	CBC & Skills	Skills
Integrity	CBC & Clinical Exam	CBC & Integrity	Integrity
Task Orientation	N/A	CBC & Skills	Skills

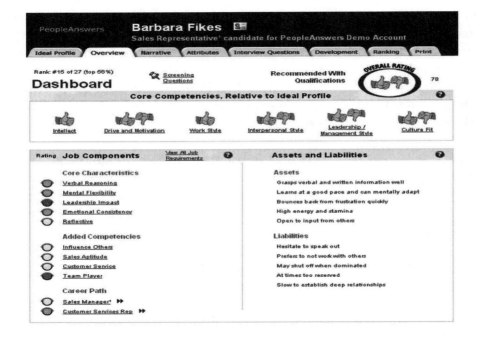

Copyright 2005 PeopleAnswers, Inc. For more information on PeopleAnswers, visit www.peopleanswers.com.

Behavioral Interview to IPC Fit

By this point, you should have an emerging shortlist of candidates, all with potential for success. You have weeded some out with the prescreening process and even more with the test. We have done this with little effort on your part, which is a surprise to many. But all of this is about to change, as the high-value activity is about to begin. You may now move on to the interview.

From the testing process (and the resume), we should be able to clearly see which candidates are best suited for the position and for the company. Now we need to dig in and start to refine this list solely for ourselves, rather than relying on outside sources. Furthermore, we should be able to clearly determine which candidate is best suited for the position, above all else. The assessment tool you used should have defined areas of solid-match characteristics and areas of vulnerability. We will use this information now as we begin to interview.

Every time I make a presentation, I start with one question: "Who has formal interview training?" Invariably, about 10% of the participants raise their hands. (HR groups tend to run closer to 50%, which is still surprisingly low.) I then ask how they learned to interview. Would you care to guess the answer? They learned from being interviewed. I essentially taught myself to ski with guidance from my father, who taught himself how to ski. The result is that neither of us really knows how to ski. Instead, we know how to "bomb" down the mountain without any notable form or control. This is not quite the mark of an expert. I am currently taking lessons to undo this flawed approach to skiing. If you haven't had any interview training, I hope you will do the same.

There are two basic types of interviews: unstructured and structured. I am a fan of the latter and a firm believer that the former is an excuse for laziness. An unstructured interview is simply a conversation with the candidate that is more or less a "free flow" or "stream of consciousness" approach. Unless you are a trained psychologist, very skilled and know precisely what to look for, I would not advise this approach. Psychologists often have a loose structure or skeleton, if you will, that they can follow, but there are clear markers they are looking for and can recognize. Anyone without training who claims to do the same thing is undoubtedly faking it.

A structured interview, however, is just as the name implies: planned and methodical. The most common example of a structured process is called a "behavioral interview," which focuses on extracting situations from candidates that fully illustrate their qualifications for a job. Since we are focusing on specific incidents from a candidate's background, the likelihood of an honest answer increases. It is easy to answer a question in the manner we believe to be the "right answer," but much harder to make up a situation "on the fly" that matches the scenario the interviewer seeks.

For example, when I hire salespeople, I know persistence is a key driver of success. I also know persistence is a relative thing, and the timeframe or degree to which someone will persist is critical. A classic unstructured interview question is: "Are you a persistent person? How?" By contrast, a behavioral question would be structured as follows: "Give me a situation in which your persistence was the key to your success." Once candidates begin their answers, demand more and more details. Keep diving deeper until you can actually visualize the situation yourself. Once you have visualized it, move on to the next topic. Every once in a while, revisit the persistence question and drill deeper. This makes it very difficult for the candidate to provide untrue or exaggerated details. And if you keep returning to a question, it gives you a chance to match details the candidate gave you earlier.

Behavioral interviewing is really a powerful instrument in the screening process. I would encourage you to read _Topgrading_ by Bradford D. Smart. In addition to being a great read on managing performance, Brad has a section on behavioral interviewing in which he lays out, in exhaustive detail, how to do it right. You can also use his training tools for your staff. There are also services available to perform behavioral interviewing if you don't like or feel comfortable doing it yourself. However you get it done, use the information. Interviewing on the fly will eradicate all of the great work you have done to this point, so don't get sloppy now. For a quick start, use the interview worksheet on the following page.

Figure 19-6

Interview Worksheet

What are the three critical areas, as determined by the IPC Profile?

1.

2.

3.

Create two structured interview questions for each area.

Example:

The three critical areas from the IPC Profile are:
1.)   Persistence
2.)   Energy
3.)   Numerical Reasoning

Persistence Questions:
   1.)   Have you ever been in a situation that required a great deal of persistence? Describe this situation to me. What period of time did it cover? How did you feel when going through the process? What was the outcome?
   2.)   Have you ever been in a situation where you later felt that you quit too soon? Describe the situation. Looking back, what would you have done differently? Why did you quit at the time?

Remember: Keep going back for more detail until you can fully envision the situation.

"Real" Reference-Checking

When we were discussing prospecting, we talked a lot about reference-checking and the manner in which we can use it to build your pipeline. Now we are going to examine it from a candidate qualification perspective. Remember the discussion about individuals who believe references are no longer useful because companies won't provide the information you need? This may be true if you don't know how to secure references, but those who can do so will find a wealth of information.

Recruiters are successful when they know the difference between a provided reference and a hidden reference. A provided reference is exactly what the name implies: a reference given by the candidate. Basically, these are useful in only one way: they are a starting point. Think of reference-checking as a private investigator would. If you want to know about me, would you ask only the people I told you to ask? I hope not, because you would discover only what I want you to discover. Real reference-checkers know these provided references are merely a starting point for gaining the meaty information.

Check the references the candidate provided. (You never know what you will find.) At the end of the reference call, ask if there is anyone else who can answer questions about the candidate. For example, ask about a coworker or former manager who can speak to the candidate's performance. Many references will be hesitant to give you these referrals, but some give them up easily. As with so many other things, it's a matter of asking. Set a goal of finding two "hidden" references for each candidate. Think of it as a game, and you may even identify candidates for your pipeline in the process.

When you ask for references, the candidate should provide at least one reference from every job held, as well as some type of educational verification. You want to match the timeline with job performance, so by default this requires some references that are not provided. Just keep asking, and you will get most of them.

I am frequently asked whether I believe this is wrong and/or sneaky or immoral. I believe you should tell the candidate that you are going to be checking other references and then make good on this task/threat. It's an acceptable task if candidates have nothing to hide and a threat if they do. My company has a service that does this for other companies. We ask candidates to sign a disclosure form that explains our process. It's often helpful to fax this form to hesitant hidden references so they understand you have the thumbs-up from the candidate. Every so often, a candidate bows out of the process. Mentioning a drug test will weed out a drug user and a hidden reference check will weed out someone with something to hide. That's not a bad outcome, if you ask me.

Background Checks

Background checks must be conducted, but you should *never* do them yourself. Background-checking is riddled with legal obstacles relating to privacy. There are many outside services that are well versed in laws relating to background checks, credit checks and drug tests, so let them handle this function.

As for its place in the process, I recommend doing background checks at the end of the interviewing process. When you have completed all other qualification steps and are ready to make an offer, do the background check (and credit check, if appropriate). I am not a lawyer, so I hesitate to offer legal advice, but I offer one word of caution regarding background checks: You must have a policy that lists your criteria and what you're checking, and it should be consistent for all applicants. In other words, you should not check one person's criminal history or request a drug test without doing so for all candidates. It will reek of discrimination, even if you simply forget.

Speak to your lawyer about crafting a hiring policy and make sure use of background checks is covered. Once you have received legal advice, conduct a thorough background check on all candidates before hiring anyone. Most often, you will find nothing of consequence, but when something does surface, it can be quite shocking. The one time you do find something may save you a fortune (in some cases, even more than that). We've all heard horror stories of violent workplace tragedies. Often, a simple background check could have prevented the wrong hire in the first place. Our website includes several highly recommended vendors who offer background-check services.

Pre-Close (Lockdown)

Finally, we have completed the qualification process and are ready to starting closing the deal. Like all good sales professionals, the power is often in the pre-close, and the actual close is a mere formality. Pre-closing in the recruitment arena is just as critical. I've lost count of the stories I've heard about "the one who got away": the great candidate who was methodically brought along, only to back out at the end.

Anyone who has lived through this knows the frustration. After all, this is a difficult process, and you resent having to start over (thank goodness for that pipeline). In almost every story I've heard, the hiring manager more than likely knew what would happen all along and didn't want to admit it. It happens to all of us. It has happened to me. The candidate is moving along well, but there is something missing. In response, I chose not to ask that hard question "because it may be insulting," when, in fact, I just didn't want to hear the answer.

Consider the following in the pre-close stage:

1.) Competitors

Is the candidate interviewing with anyone else? If so, who? How do you stack up against the other company? What is the competitor's timeframe for moving forward? Dig deep and ask the hard questions. It is uncomfortable to ask candidates if they are going on parallel interviews. If you are going to lose the candidate, it's best to know now and avoid the frustration later. If you have any hope of preventing the loss, sticking your head in the sand is not the way to go about it. As a bonus, you certainly are going to learn something useful about this candidate, including his sense of morality and ability to handle himself under pressure.

2.) Threats

Is there anything in the candidate's mind that is standing in the way of closing the deal? I call these items "outside threats." I once was in the final stages of qualifying for a job, and the company VP would ask me the same question at the end of every call: "If I offered this job to you today, assuming the compensation were right, is there anything standing in your way of accepting the position?" At the time, I thought it was curious that he asked me this question daily, but I answered honestly. He was just watching for changes. Personal issues come and go fast. What seems a great idea today may not be feasible tomorrow. Look for changes in tone, enthusiasm and demeanor to avoid the surprise loss at the end of the process. Monitor candidate temperament by asking the same question the VP asked me. You may get answers you don't want to hear, but it's better to know now than later. If you really want to cut to the chase, ask the candidate what's bothering him—as though you've already identified something—and just wait for an answer. This will give you more clues and help you spot their enthusiasm temperature rise or fall.

Finally, if you are thinking it in the pre-close, say it. If something does not feel right, bring it up immediately. So often, we are afraid of offending the candidate, when we should really be focused on making a successful hiring decision. A candidate who is not selected is just as successful as a candidate who has been chosen; he is still free to find the right job for himself.

Before we close our conversation regarding qualification and move on to closing, let me leave you with three words: Raise the bar. Stop sacrificing quality to get a body in the chair. A friend puts it this way: "One great equals three good." Let this be your motto when going forward, and raise the bar on your hiring standards. At the very least, an adequate pipeline will afford you the ability to make it happen. A great pipeline can almost guarantee it.

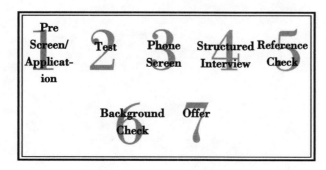

Qualifying: Summary

Hiring is not a numbers game, but a human game that must be treated as such. To hire successfully, we must focus our efforts on the Ideal Profile, using it as a measuring stick against which we evaluate candidates. To do this efficiently and effectively, our screening process must be multipronged and in-depth. Prescreening can start us off by quickly eliminating clearly unfit candidates. Testing can take us to the next level and focus our attention squarely on the high potentials. Behavioral interviewing will help us make the final selection and reference- and background-checking will verify this selection.

Lastly, we must pre-close to begin the candidate acquisition process. We are looking for potential competitors and threats that may impede our ability to get this candidate on board. All of this equals a substantive screening process that will give us the maximum chance to succeed. It is time to raise the bar, and this process can help.

Chapter 6
Close

Chapter 6
Close

If you can't figure out closing's connection to the sales cycle, something is seriously wrong. If you can't close, all of your other efforts are wasted. You have worked hard, so don't lose everything you've accomplished now. Closing should be an easy transition if you've managed the previous steps well. The pre-close should have wrapped them up, and the close should just be a formality. Let's cross the finish line.

Candidate Negotiation

This is an interesting topic because the approaches vary as widely as pay scales. I once had a client who made candidate negotiation a game. Unfortunately, it was one he lost consistently. The routine was consistent, if nothing else. First, he would offer candidates as much as 20%–30% below their minimum asking salary. Obviously, candidates would express that this was an unreasonable offer and remind the company of the minimum requirement. My client would then proceed to up the offer by a few thousand dollars. The candidate, completely insulted, would stop returning calls. Needless to say, this company is no longer a client. You are not here to haze the candidate. This is someone who will/should be working for you, and this is no way to begin their latest career endeavor with you.

In the previous chapter, I talked about the humanity in hiring. For better or worse, most people are defined in many ways by their career. Salary and title are the scorecards by which they assess their professional success. How do you think my client's approach made candidates feel? If you say "humiliated," you are correct. The ironic part of the story is that my former client intended to pay the price (or close to it) all along. It was simply a test to see if a better "deal" could be worked out with some negotiation. While one could make the case that he was testing a candidate's ability to negotiate or fend for himself in a difficult situation, I cannot agree with this approach.

Pay candidates what they're worth, and minimize negotiation to what's absolutely essential.

So often, particularly in sales, companies believe a person will be better motivated by incentives than salary or benefits. To an extent, this is true. But if you are serious about a particular candidate, you must meet the targets the person has set for themselves, assuming they are reasonable (as compared to your research). An individual who is concerned that he cannot make his mortgage payment and who accepts a commission-only compensation structure isn't someone who is making good business decisions.

You must always research market pay rates before making an offer to a candidate. Please don't guess or base salary on what you "feel" an individual is worth to you. You must "know" worth and should be able to show the numbers to an objective third party who can fully understand the logic behind them. This way, you know you are on firm ground. If, however, you believe a position is *not* worth what the market price dictates, then you may want to explore other options. Salary data research is easier than ever to find these days. Any online job board has a wealth of data to review. You can also call a local recruiting firm to see if you match up.

If the candidate's asking price is in line with the market price for his skills, offer it. One thousand dollars of extra pay equates to approximately $20 per week to an employer. If the stretch number is going to make that much of a difference in your financials, you should not be hiring in the first place because you obviously cannot afford it. Though you may grab someone for a lower price, he may feel you have taken advantage of him, and you will lose him to another company. This is a huge waste of time, money and effort.

For some strange reason, the candidate negotiation process goes even more haywire when it comes to sales. Many companies are continuously trying to get something for nothing when hiring salespeople. This is a tremendous contradiction, and it is rampant. While there are certainly some fields in which a commission-only structure is customary, not every field is suitable for this arrangement. If this is not the norm in your field, take a look at the value this candidate will deliver if they succeed. Then pull out your wallet and pay him accordingly. If this is too great a risk for you—say, you don't want to assume success for the candidate—you have either the wrong candidate or the wrong compensation structure.

I started this chapter by saying that if you fully executed the previous steps in this book, closing should be a formality. Within the context of salary negotiation, this is absolutely true. No candidate should ever be lost at the salary negotiation stage. If you lose someone here, then you missed a step (most likely in the prescreening area) or you are being cheap. I hope it's not the latter. The pre-close should be the area in which you test for money. The actual close is just the confirmation. Often, when a candidate is lost at this stage, there are competitive influences at play. This can also be remedied and assessed in the pre-close phase, and it's avoidable.

Manage the Transition/Avoid the "Back-Out"

I talked earlier about the dreaded "back-out," which occurs when a candidate is offered and accepts a position, but then decides it's no longer feasible. Back-outs are bad—very bad—and they must be avoided at all costs. They can cause desperation hires—and we know where that lands us.

While this book is not about managing talent, it is important to look at the candidate transition, or "on-boarding" process, as both recruiting and management functions. This is because back-outs occur not only pre-hire, but also within the first ninety days of employment. They are the result of the three most dangerous words in recruitment: fear, stress and reality. Place the following statement—in big letters—over your desk:

F + S + R = BACK-OUT

Have you ever eaten sausage? Most people either love it or hate it, and very few people have actually watched it being made. We are now at the stage when the sausage is getting made and the candidate (now the employee) is seeing it all—and it's not pretty. All of the smiles and pats on the back are gone. The tinsel and kazoos have been put away, and the confetti has been vacuumed off the carpet.

The recruitment honeymoon is over, and we are exposed, warts and all. The employee already fears he has made the wrong choice. After all, buyer's remorse is natural. He is learning the ropes and meeting new people, self-doubt builds, and stress starts to mount. Finally, he slips up, and the first uncomfortable situation occurs. Reality strikes. This scenario, when not carefully managed, will lead to back-outs.

I have seen it happen over and over again—often for almost negligible reasons. We once had a candidate who showed up for his first day of work to be greeted by...nothing. The manager was out sick, and no one else knew the candidate was starting on that day. After wandering around, the new employee sat alone in a conference room for four hours, went to lunch and never returned. Would you? The good news is that managing the transition from candidate to employee can be made easy.

Task Management

It is my first day of work with your company. What's the first thing I do when I arrive? If the answer has anything to do with filling out a stack of paperwork, forget it. Avoid the back-out by managing mundane tasks throughout the notification process. For example, in most cases, some time will elapse between the candidate's offer acceptance and start date. This is a perfect time to handle the paperwork—but stagger it. Every few days, have the new employee complete one more piece. Send the benefits paperwork one day, the W-2 another day and the 401K enrollment after that.

At this point, we are looking to keep the candidate engaged and look for red flags. Committed candidates generally don't drop the ball during this critical time—and if they do, there's a problem. Each time you give them a task (i.e., completing the benefits paperwork), assign a deadline. If the task comes in late, this is a red flag. Task management can be an effective early warning sign that lets you know if your new hire is wavering. If so, deal with it fast, before time is wasted and hope is lost.

Include Top Performers

During the task-management process, include some other comfort-producing elements. Your top performers can be of great help in this phase. Every few days during the transition, have a top performer or senior manager call and offer a personal welcome. If you used the success profiles that were suggested in the chapter on "positioning your product," this is particularly potent. The people you have profiled are now "famous" to this new hire and will really make them feel welcome. If you are doing the math here, this basically equates to daily contact. Our ability to welcome the new hire, while looking for red flags, is the key to avoiding a back-out.

Closing: Summary

When executed properly, closing is the natural manifestation of your successful work to date. It should not be forced; rather, it is the formal culmination to every step outlined in this book. The closing process is designed to help manage the often-bumpy transition from candidate to employee, and our worst enemy at this stage is the onset of fear, stress and reality. We can mitigate this risk with some preparation and forethought.

Task management during the on-boarding process is a great way to start. By having candidates complete the necessary paperwork throughout this notice period, we are simultaneously keeping them engaged and looking for red flags. Our top performers and senior managers will also help comfort the new hire and keep them excited about the new opportunity.

We conclude this process with a win/loss review. Debrief with others to determine what went right and what went wrong, and identify the lessons that were or could be learned. Track and analyze this data to identify patterns, and put this knowledge back into the process to raise the bar once again. Repeat, as necessary (which should be always).

I am not a big fan of "concluding" anything, whether it is a book or a final step in a process—especially when it's a living, breathing process that is always changing and growing. The fact is, at this point you have either won or lost, and it's important that I conclude this book with a question: Do you conduct a win/loss review with your salespeople? If not, you should. If you do, you know what I am talking about.

Debriefing after a candidate is won or lost is a major step in continually improving your process and, by extension, the caliber of people you are hiring. A win/loss review can be as simple as a debrief meeting to discuss what went right and what went wrong in the process. Did we see anything unusual? Are there any trends that are developing? What are they—and how and when should we respond to them? What did we learn that could be leveraged at a later date? What needs to be taken into consideration now?

You must rigorously track the results of these reviews, or they will be useless. Never rely on basic memory retention. Immediately use the win/loss review worksheet to help start the dialogue, and periodically review the results. Patterns will emerge that you can use in your next recruitment effort and everyday execution. When you see these patterns, look for the holes or fix the system, and raise the bar again. If you are serious about the people you hire, it's worth the effort.

Figure 22-7

Win/Loss Review

Use this form as a guide when conducting your win/loss reviews immediately post-hire.

Candidate Name: Hire Date:

Position:

1.) Where was the candidate sourced?

2.) Any other factors that led to the candidate sourcing?

3.) What was the candidate's background?

4.) Any significant factors in the background?

5.) When considering the screening process, were there any abnormalities or lessons learned?

6.) Were there competitors at play? If yes, who?

7.) According to the candidate, what were the main factors in our win or loss?

8.) If a loss, what were the red flags?

9.) What could we have done differently? Would it have worked?

10.) If a win, did we execute correctly? If not, where were the gaps?

11.) If a win, did we uncover any information that may lead us to more candidates like this?

Our ability to effectively recruit and deliver talent to our company is the biggest sale we can make. It will define our company for decades to come and perhaps dictate the success of your career. If you started with this visceral belief, this book was written for you. By employing some of the tools I have outlined, you will begin to see the results you desire, both personally and professionally.

Salespeople cannot succeed without a clearly defined target and plan—and neither can recruiters. Define your target, and use the definition to position your product. Build a pipeline to ensure that a steady, vibrant stable of talent is ready to go if you need to begin qualifying. And qualify with discipline and rigor. Don't compromise on finding the right person. To truly succeed, you must continually raise the bar on the talent coming into your company. After all, your success depends on it.

It has been my pleasure writing this for you, and I look forward to hearing about your success. Please keep me posted on what works (and what doesn't) and the creative ideas that work for you.

All the Best,

Greg Moran

Talent Management Group Information

Talent Management Group works with companies to implement the strategies detailed in this book. Our primary mission is to assist organizations in building their next generation of talent … today. If you are interested in any of the services listed below, please contact us at 518-261-1408 or by email at greg@talentmgtgroup.com.

- Hire, Fire and The Walking Dead Keynote Speaking and onsite training (keynote speaking or 2-hour onsite training with your field managers)

- Hire, Fire and The Walking Dead Management Workshops (half-day with your management team at your location)

- Executive Search (management and executive-level search services)

- Interview Training (behavioral-based interview training for your managers)

- Interview Outsourcing (Our trained specialists will provide behavioral-based interviewing for your candidates.)

- Reference Checking ("real" reference-checking, as detailed in the book)

- Testing and Assessment (world-class behavioral assessment technology for your business)

Index

advertising, 60, 57
  direct, 60-62
  matrix, 70
  newspaper, 62
  nontraditional, 67
  online, 63
  radio/TV, 65
  strategy. See also marketing
  top-notch, 60
  trade publications, 66
background checks, 105-108, 117
behavior, 7
  business attitude, 19
  interview. 101
  personality, 17
  tactics, 7
branding, 42-45, 51
  brand promise, 42
  develop brand, 43
  exercise, 45
business, 19, 21, 26-27, 42-49
  advertising, 26, 35, 61, 68, 70
  conventional, 19
  progressive, 19
candidate, 24
  attracting and acquiring, 33
  competitor, 28
  ideal, 24
  negotiation, 111
  talent, 27
  worksheet, 27
career, 49
  sell sheet, 49
competitiveness, 20
  incentives, 20
  landscape, 26
  supportive, 20
differentiation, 34
  worksheet, 37
elevator pitch, 38-41, 51, 71, 73
  exercise, 40
  for target group, 39
  in recruitment, 38
  sample, 41
environment, 21
  casual, 21

fast-paced, 22
  serious, 21
  slow-paced, 22
  unstructured, 21
headhunters, 83, 88
  longevity, 84
  methodology, 83
  retainer versus contingency, 84
  specialty, 83
Hire, 91
  application, 94, 95
  decisions, 91
  human game, 93
  interview, 95
  prescreen, 95
  qualifications, 91
  testing and assessment, 98
human resources, 3
  perspective, 73
IPC 15
  cultural fit, 18, 22
  intellect, 15-18, 24, 28, 94
  personality, 17
  profile, 14, 26
IQ 16
  intellect, 16
jobs, 64
  general job boards, 64
  local/regional job boards, 65
  specialized job boards, 64
management, 6, 37, 45, 62,113-115
  manager, 92
  responsibility, 6
  task management, 114
  transition, 113
market, 13-19, 44, 74, 99, 112
  define, 28
  product, 5
  target, 13
marketing, 57, 60, 62, 81, 86
  campaign strategy, 57
  ongoing, 86
  professional, 57
network, 71-73, 79, 88
  business cards, 72
  resume farming, 73

THIS BOOK DOESN'T STOP AT THE LAST PAGE!

We want to hear from you!

Join our email list to continue your experience.

WBusiness Book is not just a business book publisher, it's a community for business readers who learn and share their experiences.   Sign up for our mailing list at **www.Wbusinessbooks.com** and join the WBusiness Community.